TO YOUR HEALTH

To Your Health

Recipes for
Healthy Living
from
Lahey Clinic

TO YOUR HEALTH

Recipes for Healthy Living from Lahey Clinic

Copyright © 2000
Lahey Clinic
41 Mall Road
Burlington, Massachusetts 01805-0105
781-744-8257

Lahey Clinic Cookbook Director: Lisa G. Polacke
Photography: Larry Zimmerman
Food Specialist: John R. Di Sessa, C.E.C.
Nutritional Advisors: Mary Ann Boyle, MS, RD, CDE
Rebecca Bradley, MS, RD, CDE
Eileen Carroll, RD
Debbie Cerra Beccia, RD
Lois Maurer, MS, RD, CDE
Consultants: Jesus Perez, M.D., John Przybylski, M.D.
Support Staff: Lucille Lyons, Phil Targett, C.E.C.

Library of Congress Number: 99-098144
ISBN: 0-9675729-1-6

Designed, Edited, and Manufactured by Favorite Recipes® Press
an imprint of

FRP

P.O. Box 305142, Nashville, Tennessee 37230
800-358-0560

Project Manager: Debbie Van Mol, RD
Art Director: Steve Newman
Book Design: Brad Whitfield, Susan Breining

Manufactured in the United States of America
First Printing: 2000   12,500 copies

Material attributed to *The American Dietetic Association's Complete Food & Nutrition Guide*
(see Bibliography, page 185) is adapted by permission of John Wiley & Sons, Inc.

Nutritional information edited by Lahey Clinic.

Cover Photograph Recipes (clockwise): *Fruitful Flan,* page 168;
Cold Cucumber and Yogurt Soup, page 38;
Grilled Salmon with Pineapple Mango Salsa, page 128

DEDICATION

Those of us who fear it is too late to make changes in our lives could take a lesson from Dr. Sara M. Jordan. Dr. Jordan was one of the four founding physicians of Lahey Clinic who helped shape its future.

Medicine, however, except as an unfulfilled dream, was not part of Dr. Jordan's early life. Discouraged from pursuing a medical career because she was a woman, Dr. Jordan devoted herself to philology (the study of words) instead. After graduating from Radcliffe in 1904, she moved to Germany, obtained a doctorate in philology from the University of Munich, married, and gave birth to her only child, Mary Stuart.

It was not until the beginning of World War I in 1914 that she moved back to the United States. There, a few weeks before her 33rd birthday, she enrolled in Tufts Medical School. She had been accepted at Harvard, but Harvard reconsidered admitting a female medical student.

She worked her way through medical school, received her medical degree, and opened her own practice in 1922. One year later, Dr. Frank Lahey invited her to join his new Clinic.

Over a span of 35 years as a member of the Lahey Clinic staff, Dr. Jordan went from working side-by-side with Dr. Lahey to becoming Chairman of the Department of Gastroenterology, amid a growing staff of specialists. Dr. Jordan was highly regarded in her chosen field, and served two terms as president of the American Gastroenterological Association, the first woman to be elected to this position.

At the age of 74, she retired from Lahey Clinic, having earned the highest accolades from her medical colleagues and her devoted patients. Throughout her entire career, the philosophy of good health was the abiding concern of Dr. Jordan. She believed the key to good health was a balanced diet and exercise. Because of Dr. Jordan's contribution to health care and wellness, we dedicate this cookbook to her. Its contents are a reflection of Dr. Jordan's philosophy, and will provide you with information and recipes that will ensure healthier eating and overall wellness.

More Than Seventy-Five Years of Excellence

■

Frank Lahey was already a prominent surgeon when he gave up his positions on the Harvard and Tufts Medical School faculties and opened a small clinic in his converted apartment located in Boston's Back Bay. Chartered in 1923, the original Clinic consisted of only four physicians, but at a time when doctors tended to work in solo practice, it was an innovation—a group of physicians of differing specialties working as a team in a private setting.

From this beginning grew Lahey Clinic…today a world-renowned institution whose 500 physicians and 3,500 nurses, therapists, technicians, and other staff represent virtually every specialty and subspecialty of medicine, from allergies to cardiac surgery. Lahey today remains firmly grounded in Dr. Lahey's commitment to excellence in medical services delivered with dignity and compassion.

Thanks to its founder's emphasis on innovation and his skill at picking extraordinary associates, the Clinic has experienced continuous and significant growth. In 1926, the group moved into several Edwardian townhouses in Boston. In the following decades the building was doubled in size several times to accommodate the growing practice. Among the original members was one of Dr. Lahey's former medical students, Sara Jordan, who during her lifelong service at the Clinic became one of the world's preeminent gastroenterologists. Frank Lahey himself was a pioneer in surgery of the thyroid gland, and the Clinic staff established a strong reputation for surgery of the liver, gallbladder, bile duct, and other organs.

As Lahey Clinic's reputation grew, patients came from throughout the world as well as throughout Boston—rich and poor, famous and unknown. Celebrity patients included world leaders, performers, and athletes of the day—comedian Jimmy Durante, actor Claude Raines, golfer Bobby Jones. When President Franklin D. Roosevelt was ailing, Dr. Lahey was called in as a consultant. In 1953, British foreign minister Sir Anthony Eden was flown to Boston for emergency bile duct surgery performed by Clinic surgeon Richard B. Cattell, with Dr. Frank Lahey assisting. Throughout his life, Sir Anthony Eden returned to the Clinic for care, and served as a Trustee. Today, corporate and political leaders of international stature quietly visit the Clinic for their care.

Dr. Lahey died in 1953, and in 1963 the Clinic was organized into a nonprofit foundation, continuing to be based on Commonwealth Avenue. By the late 1960s, the Clinic had grown to a staff of about eighty physicians, located in buildings scattered throughout the Kenmore Square area. During all of its Boston days, Lahey Clinic relied on the inpatient resources of several Boston hospitals, notably New England Baptist Hospital and New England Deaconess Hospital. Clearly, the Clinic needed a new facility with its own hospital resources. The result was Lahey Clinic Medical Center in Burlington, Massachusetts, which opened in 1980. In its new home, Lahey's staff continued to innovate, pioneering in such areas as endoscopy and the use of lasers in surgery. Lahey's magnetic resonance imaging (MRI) system and its extracorporeal shock wave lithotripter (to dissolve kidney stones without surgery) were among the first in New England. With the advantage of a new medical center encompassing a large ambulatory care center and a 249-bed hospital in one structure, managed by one organization, Lahey Clinic became a model for efficient, cost-effective provision of care.

As managed care concepts began to take hold in the 1990s in Massachusetts, Lahey Clinic began development of an integrated system of physician practices providing primary care services at the community level, backed by the complex specialty resources of the medical center in Burlington, Massachusetts. In 1994, Lahey Clinic Northshore at Peabody was opened as a regional medical center to serve communities north of Boston.

Today, Lahey Clinic provides adult, pediatric, and family practice primary care in more than thirty sites throughout eastern Massachusetts, from Amesbury on the New Hampshire border to Fitchburg in Boston's far-western suburbs to Fall River in the state's southeastern corner. These practices are backed by both Lahey Clinic Medical Center in Burlington and Lahey Clinic Northshore in Peabody. In addition, Lahey Clinic has established a partnership with WorldClinic, a global telemedicine group, to provide top-quality medical care twenty-four hours a day to corporations and to business executives doing business worldwide. WorldClinic will utilize the services and expertise of Lahey Clinic's physicians and specialists to serve business travelers, working or vacationing in foreign countries.

Today, with teaching programs for the Tufts and Harvard Medical Schools, approximately fifty medical students are serving clinical rotations at Lahey Clinic Medical Center, and one hundred new physicians are receiving specialty training in residency or fellowship programs. Research at Lahey is extensive, with more than two hundred clinical trial protocols currently underway. In areas as diverse as cancer care, cardiology and cardiovascular surgery, live liver transplantation, interventional neuroradiology, colon and rectal surgery, diagnostic imaging, gastroenterology, radiation oncology, and urology, Lahey Clinic clinicians are in the forefront of medical expertise.

Lahey Clinic has been the site of many "firsts" in medicine. Among their medical innovations through the decades, Lahey staff have:

- Advanced the development of safe and effective techniques of radiation therapy for cancer
- Invented the first portable chemotherapy infusion pump for cancer patients
- Pioneered the safe use of frozen blood in surgery
- Developed one of the first heart-lung machines
- Pioneered electron beam therapy for the skin disorder mycosis fungoides
- Developed international leadership in management of Crohn's Disease and other inflammatory bowel disorders
- Pioneered techniques of angioplasty and intravenous ablation of diseased coronary arteries
- Pioneered the use of laser surgery for head and neck cancer
- Performed the first successful single-stage aortic implant
- Performed the first transplantation of fetal pig brain cells into the brain of a patient with Parkinson's disease
- Developed renal vascular surgery techniques to restore kidney function
- Developed techniques for creating new bladders for patients with bladder cancer
- Developed a digital biplane angiography program for stroke intervention and aneurysm repair

LAHEY CLINIC'S CAMPAIGN FOR CANCERCARE

*Proceeds from the sale of **To Your Health** will benefit
continuing advancement in cancer care and research at Lahey Clinic.*

■

Cancer, for all the heartache it can bring, also harbors a hidden virtue:
it binds together the human family. Researchers, physicians, patients, families,
and friends of anyone who has had cancer all share a common desire to advance
our understanding of cancer and improve our ability to prevent, detect,
and treat this disease.

At Lahey Clinic, we are harnessing that desire in our state-of-the-art
Center for CancerCare. The Clinic's Center for CancerCare will enable us
to enhance our leadership in providing cancer patients with unparalleled levels of
coordinated, compassionate care, while strengthening our role as an important
resource for cancer prevention, screening, diagnosis, and education.

From its very beginning more than seventy-five years ago, Lahey Clinic
has distinguished itself through its multidisciplinary approach to patient care.
Lahey physicians and other professionals work in close collaboration to
coordinate the care they provide for each patient. Nowhere is that philosophy
more important than in caring for patients with cancer, who often require
care and expertise from many specialists.

Lahey Clinic's physicians, many with national reputations,
are already making impressive progress toward advancing the art and the
science of cancer diagnosis with an emphasis on less invasive diagnostic tools.
They are also advancing cancer treatment, working toward more targeted
chemotherapy and radiation therapies and more precise surgical techniques.
The Center for CancerCare will reinvigorate their efforts.

The Center for CancerCare staff will also provide patients with something
almost as valuable as the most effective medical treatment: respect, compassion,
and human kindness. Lahey physicians, nurses, and other medical professionals
never forget that they are caring for a person, not just treating an illness.
Advances in cancer research and treatment represent one of the great hopes
of medicine today. Thank you for helping Lahey Clinic
turn those hopes into reality.

People Who Care Make Miracles Happen!

For more than 75 years, Lahey Clinic has provided superb health care to more than two million people throughout the world. The Clinic's physicians are national and international leaders who treat some of the most complicated medical and surgical cases. Lahey is also distinguished by its tradition of teamwork among specialists dedicated to treating the whole patient.

Certainly, one's diet plays a significant role in complete wellness. In this cookbook, dedicated to the memory of one of this country's preeminent gastroenterologists, Dr. Sara M. Jordan, we are pleased to present recipes that have been suggested by the Clinic's dietitians, nutritionists, and our executive chef.

We hope you enjoy the full range of these culinary delights.

David M. Barrett

David M. Barrett, M.D.
Chief Executive Officer

BEGINNINGS

Eating an abundance of vegetables, fruits, and other plant foods may protect against heart disease, stroke, diabetes, hypertension, and birth defects. Soluble fiber from grains and legumes may help lower blood cholesterol. Antioxidants in plant foods may help prevent cataracts, and carotenoids specifically appear to prevent deterioration of the retina. A plant-based diet can also contribute significantly to reducing obesity, a risk factor for cancer and other diseases.[2]

AVOCADO SALSA

INGREDIENTS

4	small tomatoes, chopped
1	ripe avocado, chopped
1	small red onion, chopped
1	fresh or canned jalapeño chile, finely chopped
1	green bell pepper, chopped
1	garlic clove, minced
2	tablespoons red wine vinegar
1	tablespoon olive oil or vegetable oil
4	drops of Tabasco sauce

METHOD

■ Combine the tomatoes, avocado, onion, chile and green pepper in a bowl and mix well.

■ Mash the garlic in a bowl. Stir in the wine vinegar, olive oil and Tabasco sauce. Add to the tomato mixture and toss to mix. Serve chilled or at room temperature with Tortilla Chips (page 15).

Yield: 4 servings

Approx Per Serving: Cal 155; Prot 2 g; Carbo 13 g; T Fat 12 g; 63% Calories from Fat; Chol 0 mg; Fiber 5 g; Sod 16mg

TORTILLA CHIPS

■

INGREDIENTS

4   (6-inch) flour tortillas   ■ Onion or garlic salt to taste

METHOD

■ Spray 1 side of each tortilla with nonstick cooking spray. Sprinkle lightly with onion or garlic salt.
■ Stack the tortillas greased side up. Cut the stack into halves, then into quarters and then into eighths. Arrange the wedges greased side up on a baking sheet sprayed with nonstick cooking spray.
■ Toast at 350 degrees for 5 minutes or until crisp and light brown.

Yield: 4 (8-chip) servings

Approx Per Serving: Cal 112; Prot 3 g; Carbo 20 g; T Fat 2 g; 16% Calories from Fat; Chol 0 mg; Fiber 1 g; Sod 134 mg

ARTICHOKE CHEESE DIP

■

INGREDIENTS

1   cup nonfat cottage cheese
2   tablespoons chopped fresh chives
2   tablespoons skim milk
1/4 teaspoon basil
1/4 teaspoon seasoned salt

■ Tabasco sauce to taste
■ Garlic powder to taste
4   canned artichoke hearts, drained, finely chopped
2   tablespoons grated Parmesan cheese

METHOD

■ Combine the cottage cheese, chives, skim milk, basil, seasoned salt, Tabasco sauce and garlic powder in a blender container. Process until smooth.
■ Combine the cottage cheese mixture, artichokes and Parmesan cheese in a bowl and mix well. Chill, covered, for 4 hours or longer. Serve with fresh vegetables.

Yield: 14 servings

Approx Per Serving: Cal 21; Prot 3 g; Carbo 2 g; T Fat <1 g; 12% Calories from Fat; Chol 1 mg; Fiber <1 g; Sod 148 mg

GUACAMOLE OLE

■

INGREDIENTS

2	ripe avocados, chopped	1	tablespoon chopped red onion
1	tablespoon fresh lemon juice	1/8	teaspoon pepper
1	small tomato, seeded, chopped, drained	1/8	teaspoon Tabasco sauce
		1/8	teaspoon salt

METHOD

■ Combine the avocados and lemon juice in a bowl and coarsely mash. Stir in the tomato, onion, pepper, Tabasco sauce and salt gently.

■ Spoon into a serving bowl. Serve with tortilla chips within 1 to 2 hours of preparation.

Yield: 10 servings

Approx Per Serving: Cal 67; Prot 1 g; Carbo 4 g; T Fat 6 g; 76% Calories from Fat; Chol 0 mg; Fiber 2 g; Sod 34 mg

CRAB MEAT SPREAD

■

INGREDIENTS

16	ounces reduced-fat cream cheese	1/4	cup white wine
1/2	cup reduced-fat mayonnaise	2	tablespoons confectioners' sugar
2	(6-ounce) cans lump crab meat, drained, flaked	1	teaspoon dry mustard
		1	garlic clove, minced

METHOD

■ Beat the cream cheese in a mixing bowl at medium speed until smooth. Stir in the mayonnaise, crab meat, white wine, confectioners' sugar, dry mustard and garlic. Spoon into a baking dish.

■ Bake at 350 degrees until heated through. Serve hot with assorted party crackers or toasted pita wedges.

Yield: 20 servings

Approx Per Serving: Cal 89; Prot 5 g; Carbo 3 g; T Fat 6 g; 62% Calories from Fat; Chol 26 mg; Fiber <1 g; Sod 151 mg

GRILLED BABA GHANOUSH

■

INGREDIENTS

6   (6-inch) pita bread rounds, split
2   (1-pound) unpeeled eggplant, cut lengthwise
    into halves
1   garlic clove
1/4   cup tahini
3   tablespoons fresh lemon juice
1/2   teaspoon salt
1/4   teaspoon paprika

METHOD

■ Cut each pita half into 4 wedges. Arrange the wedges in a
single layer on a baking sheet. Bake at 400 degrees for 8 to
10 minutes or until brown.

■ Arrange the eggplant cut side up on a grill rack sprayed
with nonstick cooking spray. Grill over medium-hot coals
for 20 minutes or until tender. Cool slightly. Peel the
eggplant.

■ Place the garlic in a food processor fitted with a steel blade.
Pulse until the garlic is finely chopped. Add the eggplant,
tahini, lemon juice and salt. Process until smooth. Spoon
into a serving bowl.

■ Chill, covered, until serving time. Sprinkle with the
paprika. Serve with the pita chips.

Yield: 12 (1/4-cup) servings and 48 pita chips

*Approx Per 1/4 Cup and 4 Pita Chips: Cal 134; Prot 5 g;
Carbo 22 g; T Fat 3 g; 22% Calories from Fat; Chol 0 mg;
Fiber 3 g; Sod 261 mg*

■

*While most of us resist
overwhelming changes in
life, we are not averse to
making dietary adjustments
at our own pace—
particularly when the
potential benefits are so
great. Start slowly to insure
permanent results. When
you are used to one change,
try for more. Here are some
hints to help you on your
way. Small meat portions
tend to work best mixed
with lots of vegetables and
grains. Try stir-fries, pastas,
soups and stews, burritos,
casseroles, and main dish
salads. These dishes are a
great opportunity to try
alternatives to meat as
well, like beans, tofu, nuts,
and seeds. Keep some of
your favorite fruits on
hand for snacks when
you are hungry.[2]*

SPICY PITA CRISPS

5 (5-inch) pita rounds,
split
1 tablespoon oregano
1 tablespoon basil
1 teaspoon garlic powder
1 teaspoon dillweed

Spray each side of the
pita rounds with butter-
flavor nonstick cooking
spray. Cut each round
into 6 wedges.

Combine the oregano,
basil, garlic powder and
dillweed in a sealable
plastic bag and seal
tightly. Shake to mix.
Add the pita wedges and
shake to coat.

Arrange the pita wedges
in a single layer on a
baking sheet. Bake at
350 degrees for 5 to
8 minutes or until light
brown and crisp.

Yield: 60 crisps

MUSHROOM PATE

INGREDIENTS

8   ounces fresh mushrooms, chopped
1   tablespoon margarine
1/4 cup chopped scallions
1 1/2 teaspoons chopped garlic
1/3 cup chicken broth
1   tablespoon margarine, softened
4   ounces reduced-fat cream cheese, softened
2   tablespoons chopped fresh chives
■   Salt and freshly ground pepper to taste

METHOD

■ Sauté the mushrooms in 1 tablespoon margarine in a
nonstick skillet over medium heat for 2 to 3 minutes. Stir
in the scallions and garlic.

■ Sauté for 1 minute. Stir in the broth. Cook over high heat
until all the liquid has evaporated, stirring frequently. Cool
to room temperature.

■ Combine 1 tablespoon margarine and cream cheese in a
mixing bowl. Beat at medium speed until smooth. Stir in
the mushroom mixture, chives, salt and pepper. Spoon into
a serving bowl.

■ Chill, covered, until serving time. Garnish with additional
chopped chives. Serve with toast points.

Yield: 8 (2-tablespoon) servings

*Approx Per Serving: Cal 69; Prot 3 g; Carbo 3 g; T Fat 5 g;
68% Calories from Fat; Chol 8 mg; Fiber <1 g; Sod 108 mg*

CRANBERRY RELISH SPREAD

∎

INGREDIENTS

24 ounces reduced-fat cream cheese, softened
2 cups fresh cranberries
3/4 cup sugar

3/4 teaspoon grated orange zest
1/3 cup orange juice
1/2 teaspoon grated lemon zest
1 1/2 tablespoons lemon juice

METHOD

∎ Spread the cream cheese in an 8-inch springform pan. Chill, covered, for 8 hours.
∎ Mix the remaining ingredients in a saucepan. Bring to a boil, stirring occasionally; reduce heat. Cook over medium heat for 3 minutes or until the cranberries pop, stirring occasionally. Let stand until cool. Chill, covered, for 8 hours or longer.
∎ Arrange the springform pan on a serving platter; remove the side. Drain the cranberry mixture and spoon over the cream cheese. Serve with gingersnaps.

Yield: 24 servings

Approx Per Serving: Cal 95; Prot 3 g; Carbo 10 g; T Fat 5 g; 47% Calories from Fat; Chol 16 mg; Fiber <1 g; Sod 84 mg

CLASSIC HUMMUS

∎

INGREDIENTS

1 (15-ounce) can garbanzos
1 1/2 small garlic cloves, minced
2 1/2 tablespoons tahini

2 tablespoons fresh lemon juice
1 1/2 tablespoons water

METHOD

∎ Drain the beans, reserving 1/4 cup of the liquid. Combine the beans, reserved liquid, garlic, tahini, lemon juice and water in a food processor container.
∎ Process for 3 minutes or until smooth. Spoon into a serving bowl. Serve with pita chips and/or fresh vegetables.

Yield: 6 (1/4-cup) servings

Approx Per Serving: Cal 124; Prot 5 g; Carbo 18 g; T Fat 5 g; 31% Calories from Fat; Chol 0 mg; Fiber 4 g; Sod 214 mg

DILLED SALMON MOUSSE

INGREDIENTS

1	envelope unflavored gelatin	1	tablespoon fresh lemon juice
1/2	cup clam juice	1	tablespoon minced onion
1/2	cup 1% cottage cheese	1/8	teaspoon Tabasco sauce
1	to 2 tablespoons 1% milk	1	(15-ounce) can sockeye salmon, drained, finely flaked
3/4	cup plain nonfat yogurt		Red leaf lettuce
1/3	cup finely chopped celery		
2	tablespoons chopped fresh dillweed		

METHOD

■ Sprinkle the gelatin over the clam juice in a saucepan. Let stand for 5 minutes. Cook over medium heat until the gelatin dissolves, stirring occasionally. Let stand until cool.

■ Process the cottage cheese and 1% milk in a blender container until of the desired consistency. Stir the cottage cheese mixture, yogurt, celery, dillweed, lemon juice, onion and Tabasco sauce into the gelatin mixture. Fold in the salmon.

■ Spoon the salmon mixture into a 4-cup mold sprayed with nonstick cooking spray. Chill, covered, for 3 hours or until set.

■ Invert the mold onto a lettuce-lined serving platter. Serve with assorted party crackers and/or fresh vegetables.

Yield: 16 (1/4-cup) servings

Approx Per Serving: Cal 55; Prot 7 g; Carbo 2 g; T Fat 2 g; 34% Calories from Fat; Chol 12 mg; Fiber <1 g; Sod 199 mg

Hot Tomato Spread

■

INGREDIENTS

1   medium onion, chopped
2   garlic cloves, minced
2   tablespoons butter or margarine
1   tomato, chopped
8   ounces reduced-fat cream cheese, softened, or Mock
    Cream Cheese (below)
3   tablespoons sugar

METHOD

■ Sauté the onion and garlic in the butter in a skillet until tender. Add the tomato. Cook until the tomato is tender, stirring frequently. Add the cream cheese and sugar and mix well. Spoon into a serving bowl. Serve hot with assorted party crackers.

Yield: 8 servings

Approx Per Serving: Cal 119; Prot 4 g; Carbo 9 g; T Fat 8 g; 59% Calories from Fat; Chol 24 mg; Fiber <1 g; Sod 115 mg

Mock Cream Cheese

■

INGREDIENTS

1   cup reduced-fat cottage cheese
1/4 cup tub-style margarine
2   tablespoons skim milk

METHOD

■ Mix the cottage cheese and margarine in a bowl. Stir in skim milk until of the desired consistency.

Yield: 8 (2-tablespoon) servings

Approx Per Serving: Cal 68; Prot 4 g; Carbo 1 g; T Fat 5 g; 66% Calories from Fat; Chol 1 mg; Fiber 0 g; Sod 153 mg

■

You'll find plenty of reduced-fat and fat-free choices on supermarket shelves, for example, fat-free salad dressings and low-fat ice cream. Be aware that many lower-fat processed foods have the same amount or more total calories than their traditional counterparts. You'll want to read the Nutrition Facts panel on the food label to compare.[4]

TOMATO PESTO SPREAD

INGREDIENTS

2	cups plain nonfat yogurt
1	ounce sun-dried tomatoes
3/4	cup boiling water
3	garlic cloves, minced
1/4	cup chopped fresh parsley
1/3	cup freshly grated Parmesan cheese
2	tablespoons slivered almonds, toasted
1	teaspoon basil
2	teaspoons vegetable oil

METHOD

- Place a colander in a 2-quart glass measure or medium bowl. Line the colander with 4 layers of cheesecloth, letting the cheesecloth extend over the edge. Spoon the yogurt into the prepared colander. Chill, covered loosely with plastic wrap, for 12 hours. Spoon the yogurt cheese into a bowl. Chill, covered, in the refrigerator.
- Combine the sun-dried tomatoes and boiling water in a heatproof bowl. Let stand for 10 minutes; drain.
- Combine the sun-dried tomatoes, garlic, parsley, Parmesan cheese, almonds, basil and oil in a food processor container. Pulse until minced. Chill, covered, in the refrigerator.
- Combine the yogurt cheese and sun-dried tomato mixture in a bowl and mix well. Shape into a ball and place on a serving platter. Garnish with sprigs of fresh parsley. Serve with assorted party crackers.

Yield: 6 (1/4-cup) servings

Approx Per Serving: Cal 103; Prot 7 g; Carbo 10 g; T Fat 5 g; 37% Calories from Fat; Chol 6 mg; Fiber 1 g; Sod 155 mg

BLACK BEAN BURRITOS

■

INGREDIENTS

1	tablespoon chili powder	1	(15-ounce) can black beans, drained, rinsed, mashed
1	tablespoon vegetable oil	1	(4-ounce) can chopped green chiles, drained
1	teaspoon cumin		
1/4	teaspoon oregano	8	(8-inch) flour tortillas
1/4	teaspoon salt	1	cup shredded reduced-fat Monterey Jack cheese
1/2	small onion, finely chopped		
1/2	green bell pepper, chopped		
2	garlic cloves, minced		

METHOD

■ Combine the chili powder, oil, cumin, oregano and salt in a microwave-safe dish. Microwave, covered, on High for 1 minute. Stir in the onion, green pepper and garlic.

■ Microwave, covered, on High for 1 to 2 minutes or until the onion is tender, stirring ever 30 seconds. Add the beans and chiles and mix well.

■ Spread 1/4 cup of the bean mixture down the center of each tortilla and sprinkle with 2 tablespoons of the cheese. Roll to enclose the filling.

■ Arrange the tortillas seam side down in a 7×11-inch microwave-safe dish. Cover with 4 damp paper towels. Microwave on High for 1 1/2 minutes; rotate the dish 1/2 turn. Microwave for 1 1/2 to 2 1/2 minutes longer or until heated through. Cut each tortilla into halves.

Yield: 16 servings

Approx Per Serving: Cal 133; Prot 6 g; Carbo 18 g; T Fat 4 g; 28% Calories from Fat; Chol 4 mg; Fiber 3 g; Sod 368 mg

TANDOORI CHICKEN SKEWERS

◼

INGREDIENTS

1   onion, chopped
$^1/_4$ cup plain reduced-fat yogurt
1   tablespoon olive oil
1   garlic clove, chopped
$^1/_2$ teaspoon minced gingerroot
$^1/_2$ teaspoon coriander
$^1/_4$ teaspoon salt

$^1/_4$ teaspoon turmeric
$^1/_4$ teaspoon cumin
$^1/_4$ teaspoon black pepper
$^1/_4$ teaspoon red pepper
$1^1/_2$ pounds boneless skinless chicken
      breasts, cut into $^1/_2$-inch strips
2   limes, sliced

METHOD

◼ Combine the onion, yogurt, olive oil, garlic, gingerroot, coriander, salt, turmeric, cumin, black pepper and red pepper in a food processor container. Process until smooth.

◼ Pour the yogurt mixture over the chicken in a large heavy-duty sealable plastic bag and seal tightly. Toss to coat. Marinate in the refrigerator for 2 hours, turning occasionally.

◼ Drain the chicken, discarding the marinade. Thread the chicken onto 24 skewers. Arrange the skewers in a single layer on a broiler rack sprayed with nonstick cooking spray. Place the rack in a broiler pan. Broil for 6 minutes per side or until the chicken is cooked through. Arrange the skewers on a serving platter. Top with the lime slices.

Yield: 24 skewers

Approx Per Skewer: Cal 41; Prot 6 g; Carbo 1 g; T Fat 1 g; 29% Calories from Fat; Chol 16 mg; Fiber <1 g; Sod 40 mg
Nutritional information includes the entire amount of marinade.

CRAB PUFFS

■

INGREDIENTS

1	(7-ounce) can crab meat, drained
1/2	cup (1 stick) margarine, softened
1	(5-ounce) jar Cheddar cheese spread
1 1/2	teaspoons mayonnaise
1/2	teaspoon garlic powder
1/2	teaspoon seasoned salt
6	English muffins, split

METHOD

■ Combine the crab meat, margarine, cheese spread, mayonnaise, garlic powder and seasoned salt in a bowl and mix well.

■ Spread each muffin half with some of the crab meat mixture. Arrange on a baking sheet.

■ Bake at 400 degrees for 15 to 20 minutes or until brown and bubbly. Cut each muffin half into 6 wedges. Arrange on a serving platter.

Yield: 72 wedges

Approx Per Wedge: Cal 30; Prot 1 g; Carbo 2 g; T Fat 2 g; 53% Calories from Fat; Chol 3 mg; Fiber <1 g; Sod 71 mg

■

Increase your daily water intake by taking water breaks during the day instead of coffee breaks. When you walk by a water fountain, always take a drink, whether you are thirsty or not. At snack time, refresh yourself with juice, milk, or sparkling water.[4]

LAMB AND VEGETABLE KABOBS

■

INGREDIENTS

2   pounds boneless leg of lamb, trimmed

¼   cup red wine vinegar

■   Juice of 2 lemons

¼   cup minced fresh parsley

½   teaspoon cumin

½   teaspoon pepper

¼   teaspoon salt

3   garlic cloves, minced

1   unpeeled medium eggplant

1   (8-ounce) zucchini

1   large onion, cut into 8 wedges

1   large red bell pepper, cut into 8 chunks

1   large green bell pepper, cut into 8 chunks

8   large mushrooms

METHOD

■ Cut the lamb into twenty-four 2-inch cubes. Combine the wine vinegar, lemon juice, parsley, cumin, pepper, salt and garlic in a sealable plastic bag. Add the lamb and seal tightly. Toss to coat. Marinate in the refrigerator for 8 hours, turning occasionally.

■ Cut the eggplant lengthwise into quarters. Cut each quarter vertically into 4 pieces. Cut the zucchini lengthwise into halves. Cut each half vertically into 4 pieces. Thread 2 eggplant pieces, 1 zucchini piece and 1 onion wedge onto each of eight 10-inch skewers.

■ Drain the lamb, reserving the marinade. Thread 3 lamb cubes, 1 red pepper chunk, 1 green pepper chunk and 1 mushroom alternately onto each of eight 10-inch skewers.

■ Arrange the eggplant kabobs on a grill rack sprayed with nonstick cooking spray. Grill over medium-hot coals for 15 minutes, basting frequently with the reserved marinade; turn the kabobs. Grill for 7 minutes longer or until the vegetables are of the desired degree of crispness. Add the lamb kabobs to the grill rack. Grill for 4 minutes per side or until of the desired degree of doneness, basting frequently with the reserved marinade. Serve each guest 1 eggplant kabob and 1 lamb kabob.

Yield: 8 servings

Approx Per Serving: Cal 209; Prot 25 g; Carbo 12 g; T Fat 7 g; 29% Calories from Fat; Chol 73 mg; Fiber 4 g; Sod 135 mg
Nutritional information includes the entire amount of marinade.

Mushroom Cups

■

Ingredients

12   slices party bread, crusts trimmed
$1/2$ cup fine bread crumbs
2   tablespoons finely chopped fresh parsley
1   small garlic clove, minced
■   Freshly ground pepper to taste
2   teaspoons margarine
12   medium mushroom caps
$1/3$ cup shredded part-skim mozzarella cheese

Method

■ Flatten the bread with a rolling pin on a hard surface. Cut the bread into twelve $1^{1/2}$-inch rounds. Press the bread rounds into miniature baking cups. Bake at 300 degrees for 20 to 25 minutes or until light brown. Remove to a wire rack to cool.

■ Combine the bread crumbs, parsley, garlic and pepper in a food processor container. Process until mixed. Add the margarine. Process just until mixed.

■ Spoon a small amount of the crumb mixture into each mushroom cap. Sprinkle with the cheese. Place 1 stuffed mushroom cap in each baked bread cup. Arrange on a baking sheet. Bake at 400 degrees for 10 minutes. Broil for 1 minute. Serve immediately.

Yield: 12 servings

Approx Per Serving: Cal 71; Prot 4 g; Carbo 11 g; T Fat 2 g; 23% Calories from Fat; Chol 2 mg; Fiber 1 g; Sod 200 mg

---

■

In its broadest definition, being a vegetarian means eating no meat, poultry, and fish. Instead, plant sources of food—grains, legumes, nuts, vegetables, and fruits—form the basis of the diet. Lacto-ovo-vegetarians choose a diet with eggs and dairy products, but no meat, poultry, and fish. Most vegetarians in the United States fit within this group. Lacto-vegetarians avoid meat, poultry, fish, and eggs, but eat dairy products. Strict vegetarians, or vegans, follow an eating plan with no animal products.[4]

PORK TREASURES

◼

INGREDIENTS

2 tablespoons hoisin sauce
2 tablespoons soy sauce
2 tablespoons brown sugar
1 tablespoon Worcestershire sauce
1 tablespoon toasted sesame oil
1 shallot, chopped
2 teaspoons five-spice powder
2 teaspoons minced gingerroot
2 garlic cloves, minced
2 pounds pork tenderloin, cut into 3/4-inch cubes

METHOD

◼ Combine the hoisin sauce, soy sauce, brown sugar, Worcestershire sauce, sesame oil, shallot, five-spice powder, gingerroot and garlic in a bowl and mix well. Pour over the pork in a sealable plastic bag and seal tightly. Toss to coat.

◼ Marinate in the refrigerator for 8 to 12 hours, turning occasionally. Drain, discarding the marinade. Pat the pork dry with paper towels.

◼ Arrange the pork in a single layer in a shallow baking pan; do not allow the edges to touch. Bake at 350 degrees for 25 to 30 minutes or until the pork is cooked through and light brown. Serve hot with wooden picks.

Yield: 16 servings

Approx Per Serving: Cal 93; Prot 12 g; Carbo 3 g; T Fat 3 g; 30% Calories from Fat; Chol 34 mg; Fiber <1 g; Sod 232 mg Nutritional information includes the entire amount of marinade.

ASIAN PORK SATE

∎

INGREDIENTS

2	(1-pound) pork tenderloins, trimmed	2	tablespoons reduced-sodium soy sauce
½	cup reduced-sodium chicken broth	1	teaspoon Asian sesame oil
2	tablespoons creamy peanut butter	½	teaspoon crushed red pepper
¼	cup honey	1	garlic clove, minced
¼	cup hoisin sauce	¼	cup water
2	teaspoons coriander		

METHOD

▨ Cut each tenderloin lengthwise into 12 equal strips. Thread the strips onto twenty-four 6-inch skewers. Arrange the kabobs in a single layer in a shallow dish.

▨ Combine the broth, peanut butter, honey, hoisin sauce, coriander, soy sauce, sesame oil, red pepper and garlic in a bowl and mix well. Reserve ³/₄ cup of the peanut butter sauce to serve with the kabobs.

▨ Stir the water into the remaining peanut butter sauce. Pour over the kabobs, turning to coat. Marinate, covered, in the refrigerator for 30 minutes, turning 2 or 3 times.

▨ Drain the kabobs, reserving the marinade. Arrange the kabobs on a grill rack sprayed with nonstick cooking spray. Grill over medium-hot coals for 6 minutes per side or until the lamb is of the desired degree of doneness, basting occasionally with the reserved marinade. Serve the kabobs with the reserved peanut butter sauce.

Yield: 2 dozen kabobs

Approx Per Kabob: Cal 75; Prot 9 g; Carbo 5 g; T Fat 2 g; 29% Calories from Fat; Chol 23 mg; Fiber <1 g; Sod 110 mg
Nutritional information includes the entire amount of marinade.

SALMON KABOBS

■

INGREDIENTS

1/2 cup grapefruit juice
1 tablespoon minced gingerroot
2 teaspoons lime juice
1 teaspoon red wine vinegar
1/2 teaspoon canola oil
1/4 teaspoon hot pepper sauce, or
 to taste

■ Salt and freshly ground pepper
 to taste
12 ounces salmon fillets, skinned,
 cut into 1/4-inch pieces
2 or 3 small zucchini, cut into
 60 slices
■ Cucumber Yogurt Sauce

METHOD

■ Combine the grapefruit juice, gingerroot, lime juice, wine vinegar, canola oil,
 hot pepper sauce, salt and pepper in a bowl and mix well. Add the salmon and
 mix gently.
■ Marinate, covered, in the refrigerator for 30 minutes to 10 hours; drain. Thread
 1 piece of the salmon between 2 slices of zucchini on each of 30 skewers.
■ Arrange the skewers on a rack in a broiler pan. Broil for 45 seconds or just until the
 salmon is cooked through. Serve with the Cucumber Yogurt Sauce.

CUCUMBER YOGURT SAUCE

■

INGREDIENTS

1 cup plain nonfat yogurt
1/4 cup finely chopped cucumber
1/4 cup finely chopped onion
2 teaspoons olive oil

1/4 teaspoon salt
1/4 teaspoon pepper
1 garlic clove, minced

METHOD

■ Combine the yogurt, cucumber, onion, olive oil, salt, pepper and garlic in a bowl
 and mix well.
■ Spoon into a serving dish. Chill, covered, until serving time.

Yield: 30 servings

*Approx Per Kabob and 2 1/2 Teaspoons Sauce: Cal 28; Prot 3 g; Carbo 2 g; T Fat 1 g;
40% Calories from Fat; Chol 7 mg; Fiber <1 g; Sod 31 mg
Nutritional information includes the entire amount of marinade.*

CHINESE SPINACH BITES

■

INGREDIENTS

1/2   (10-ounce) package frozen chopped spinach
3   ounces egg substitute
1/2   cup finely chopped water chestnuts
1/4   cup finely chopped green bell pepper
1/4   cup finely chopped onion
1/8   teaspoon pepper

METHOD

■ Cook the spinach using package directions; drain. Press the spinach to remove the excess moisture.

■ Combine the spinach, egg substitute, water chestnuts, green pepper, onion and pepper in a bowl and mix well. Drop by teaspoonfuls onto a hot griddle.

■ Bake until brown on both sides. Arrange in a single layer on a baking sheet.

■ Chill, covered, until 30 minutes before serving time. Bake at 300 degrees for 20 to 30 minutes or until heated through. Serve with your favorite sweet-and-sour sauce.

Yield: 36 servings

Approx Per Serving: Cal 5; Prot <1 g; Carbo 1 g; T Fat <1 g; 18% Calories from Fat; Chol <1 mg; Fiber <1 g; Sod 7 mg

■

Studies show a positive link between vegetarian eating and health. In general, heart disease, high blood pressure, adult-onset diabetes, obesity, and some forms of cancer tend to develop less often among vegetarians than nonvegetarians. Vegetarians also appear to be at lower risk for osteoporosis, kidney stones, gallstones, and breast cancer.[4]

TEMPEH FAJITAS

INGREDIENTS

6	(8-inch) whole wheat or flour tortillas
1¹/₂	cups sliced onions
1	Anaheim chile, minced
1	garlic clove, chopped
2	teaspoons oregano
1¹/₂	teaspoons cumin
1	teaspoon coriander
1	teaspoon canola oil
2¹/₂	cups sliced red and green bell peppers
2	tablespoons Mexican-style red salsa
1¹/₂	cups (¹/₄×2-inch strips) tempeh

METHOD

■ Stack the tortillas and wrap tightly in foil. Heat at 300 degrees for 10 minutes or until soft, pliable and warm.

■ Sauté the onions, chile, garlic, oregano, cumin and coriander in the canola oil in a nonreactive skillet for 5 minutes. Add the bell peppers and salsa and mix well.

■ Cook, covered, over medium heat for 5 minutes, stirring occasionally. Stir in the tempeh. Cook for 3 to 4 minutes longer or until the vegetables are tender, stirring occasionally.

■ Spoon ¹/₆ of the vegetable mixture on each tortilla. Roll to enclose the filling. Serve immediately with shredded lettuce, chopped tomatoes, soy cheese and vegetarian sour cream if desired. Discard the seeds of the chile for a milder flavor.

Yield: 6 servings

Approx Per Serving: Cal 189; Prot 12 g; Carbo 33 g; T Fat 5 g; 19% Calories from Fat; Chol 0 mg; Fiber 6 g; Sod 199 mg

Turkey Puffs

■

INGREDIENTS

½ cup finely chopped cooked turkey breast	¼ teaspoon dry mustard
1½ tablespoons reduced-fat mayonnaise	¼ teaspoon curry powder
1 tablespoon dry bread crumbs	6 slices whole wheat bread
2 teaspoons minced scallions	1 egg white
½ teaspoon Worcestershire sauce	1 teaspoon paprika

METHOD

■ Combine the turkey, mayonnaise, bread crumbs, scallions, Worcestershire sauce, dry mustard and curry powder in a bowl and mix well. Chill, covered, for several hours.

■ Cut each bread slice into 4 squares. Arrange the squares in a single layer on a baking sheet. Bake at 250 degrees for 30 minutes.

■ Beat the egg white in a mixing bowl at medium speed until soft peaks form. Fold into the turkey mixture. Spread on the bread squares. Sprinkle with the paprika.

■ Bake at 500 degrees for 5 minutes. Serve immediately.

Yield: 2 dozen turkey puffs

Approx Per Turkey Puff: Cal 26; Prot 2 g; Carbo 4 g; T Fat 1 g; 22% Calories from Fat; Chol 3 mg; Fiber 1 g; Sod 51 mg

Guiltless Nog

■

INGREDIENTS

1	pint frozen vanilla nonfat yogurt	1½ to 2 tablespoons rum extract
2	cups skim milk	⅛ to ¼ teaspoon nutmeg

METHOD

■ Combine the yogurt, skim milk, flavoring and nutmeg in a blender container.
■ Process until smooth. Pour into chilled glasses.

Yield: 8 servings

Approx Per Serving: Cal 86; Prot 4 g; Carbo 14 g; T Fat <1 g; 1% Calories from Fat; Chol 1 mg; Fiber 0 g; Sod 69 mg

Cool Spiced Tea

■

INGREDIENTS

1	gallon water	3	(3-inch) cinnamon sticks, broken into halves
1	teaspoon cardamom seeds		
1	teaspoon whole allspice berries	8	tea bags

METHOD

■ Combine the water, cardamom seeds, allspice and cinnamon in a large saucepan. Bring to a boil. Remove from heat. Add the tea bags.
■ Let stand, covered, for 5 minutes. Strain the tea into a heatproof pitcher. Chill in the refrigerator.
■ Pour over ice in glasses. Garnish with sprigs of fresh mint.

Yield: 16 (1-cup) servings

Approx Per Serving: Cal 2; Prot 0 g; Carbo 1 g; T Fat 0 g; 0% Calories from Fat; Chol 0 mg; Fiber 0 g; Sod 7 mg

TEA PUNCH

■

INGREDIENTS

1   (6-ounce) can frozen lemonade
    concentrate, prepared, chilled
1   (6-ounce) can frozen orange juice
    concentrate, prepared, chilled
2   quarts herbal tea, cooled

1   orange, chilled, sliced
1   lemon, chilled, sliced
10 strawberries, sliced
8   to 10 mint leaves

METHOD

■ Combine the lemonade, orange juice, tea, orange slices, lemon slices, strawberries and mint leaves in a punch bowl and mix gently. Add the desired amount of ice cubes. Ladle into punch cups.

Yield: 18 (6-ounce) servings

Approx Per Serving: Cal 44; Prot <1 g; Carbo 11 g; T Fat <1 g; 1% Calories from Fat; Chol 0 mg; Fiber 1 g; Sod 3 mg

TINGLING PEACH SLUSHES

■

INGREDIENTS

1   (16-ounce) package frozen peaches,
    slightly thawed
1   (6-ounce) can frozen orange juice
    concentrate

1   (12-ounce) can peach nectar
1   (2-liter) bottle diet lemon-lime soda

METHOD

■ Combine the peaches, orange juice concentrate and peach nectar in a blender container. Process until smooth. Pour into ice cube trays.

■ Freeze until firm. Let stand at room temperature for 20 minutes or until slightly thawed.

■ Place 2 or 3 cubes in each of 8 glasses. Add enough soda to fill.

Yield: 8 servings

Approx Per Serving: Cal 81; Prot 1 g; Carbo 18 g; T Fat <1 g; 5% Calories from Fat; Chol 0 mg; Fiber 2 g; Sod 42 mg

GRANNY SMITH APPLE AND FENNEL SOUP

From Tasty Lite Cuisine Sodexho Marriott Services

INGREDIENTS

5	Granny Smith apples, peeled, chopped
1¼	pounds carrots, sliced
1¼	pounds onions, sliced
10	ounces fennel bulbs, coarsely chopped
5	cups chicken broth
5	cups water
1¼	cups white wine
3	bay leaves
2⅔	teaspoons ground pepper
1⅓	teaspoons thyme

METHOD

■ Sweat the apples, carrots, onions and fennel in a small amount of the broth in a stockpot. Stir in the remaining broth, water, white wine, bay leaves, pepper and thyme. Bring to a boil; reduce heat.

■ Simmer, covered, for 20 minutes, stirring occasionally. Strain the soup, reserving the liquid. Discard the bay leaves. Process the apple mixture in a blender or food processor until puréed. Add the reserved liquid and mix well. Return the soup to the saucepan.

■ Cook just until heated through, stirring occasionally. Ladle into soup bowls. Serve immediately.

Yield: 20 (1-cup) servings

Approx Per Serving: Cal 65; Prot 2 g; Carbo 11 g; T Fat 1 g; 8% Calories from Fat; Chol 0 mg; Fiber 2 g; Sod 213 mg

ARMENIAN SOUP

From Lahey Clinic Executive Chef John R. Di Sessa, C.E.C.

■

INGREDIENTS

1/4 cup minced onion
1 carrot, finely chopped
1 rib celery, finely chopped
5 cups chicken broth
2 eggs

■ Juice of 1 lemon
1/2 cup (1/2-inch pieces) vermicelli, cooked, drained, cooled
■ Salt to taste
1 tablespoon chopped fresh parsley

METHOD

■ Spray the bottom of a heavy saucepan with nonstick cooking spray. Heat until hot. Add the onion, carrot and celery.

■ Cook for 7 minutes or until the onion is tender, stirring frequently. Add the broth and mix well. Bring to a boil.

■ Cook for 10 minutes, stirring occasionally; reduce heat. Simmer for 20 minutes or until the carrot is tender, stirring occasionally; skim.

■ Whisk the eggs in a bowl until blended. Stir in the lemon juice. Stir a small amount of the hot broth mixture into the egg mixture. Stir the egg mixture into the broth mixture.

■ Cook for 5 minutes or until the eggs harden, stirring occasionally. Add the pasta and mix well. Season with salt. Ladle into soup bowls. Sprinkle with the parsley.

Yield: 4 servings

Approx Per Serving: Cal 148; Prot 12 g; Carbo 14 g; T Fat 5 g; 28% Calories from Fat; Chol 106 mg; Fiber 1 g; Sod 1019 mg

Dill Oil

2 cups chopped fresh
dillweed
Salt to taste
1/2 cup canola oil
1/2 cup olive oil

Blanch the dillweed in
boiling salted water in a
saucepan for 15 seconds;
drain. Combine with
ice water in a bowl; drain.
Press the dillweed to
remove the excess
moisture.

Combine the dillweed,
canola oil and olive oil in
a blender container.
Process for 3 to 4 minutes
or until puréed and bright
green in color. Pour into a
jar with a tight-fitting lid.
Chill for 8 to 10 hours.

Strain the oil through a
fine mesh sieve and
discard the solids. Chill
for 24 hours longer and
decant. Store, covered, in
the refrigerator.

Yield: 1 cup

Cold Cucumber and Yogurt Soup

From Lahey Clinic Executive Chef John R. Di Sessa, C.E.C.

*For a wonderful vegetarian first course, add
additional seasonal fresh vegetables.*

Ingredients

2	English cucumbers, peeled, seeded, chopped
1	cup plain nonfat yogurt
3	tablespoons fresh lemon juice
	Salt and pepper to taste
1	yellow tomato, peeled, seeded, chopped
1	tablespoon olive oil
1	cup Hot-and-Sour Cucumbers (page 40)
2	teaspoons fresh dillweed
	Freshly ground pepper to taste
2	tablespoons radish sprouts
4	teaspoons Dill Oil

Method

- Combine the cucumbers, yogurt and lemon juice in a blender container. Process until puréed. Season with salt and pepper. Chill the soup, covered, until serving time.
- Toss the tomato with the olive oil in a bowl. Season with salt and pepper.

Assembly

- Stir the soup. Ladle into 4 shallow soup bowls. Place each bowl on a serving plate.
- Spoon 1/4 of the tomato mixture into the center of each bowl and arrange 1/4 of the Hot-and-Sour Cucumbers at the 4 points around the tomato. Sprinkle with the dillweed and freshly ground pepper.
- Sprinkle with the radish sprouts and drizzle with the Dill Oil.

Yield: 4 servings

*Approx Per Serving: Cal 152; Prot 4 g; Carbo 18 g; T Fat 8 g;
46% Calories from Fat; Chol 1 mg; Fiber 2 g; Sod 52 mg*

Cold Cucumber and Yogurt Soup

39

Hot-and-Sour Cucumbers

■

Ingredients

2	English cucumbers, cut lengthwise into halves, seeded
6	ounces red onion, thinly sliced
3	ounces fennel, thinly sliced
1	jalapeño chile, chopped
1/2	teaspoon crushed pink peppercorns
1	cup rice wine vinegar
1	cup sugar
1 1/2	bay leaves

Method

■ Cut the cucumbers into thin slices. Combine the cucumbers, onion, fennel, chile and peppercorns in a bowl and mix gently.

■ Combine the wine vinegar, sugar and bay leaves in a saucepan. Bring to a simmer. Simmer for 5 minutes, stirring occasionally. Remove from heat. Let stand until cool.

■ Pour the vinegar mixture over the cucumbers and stir gently. Chill, covered, for 3 hours or longer. Discard the bay leaves.

■ May be stored, covered, in the refrigerator for up to 1 week. For spicier cucumbers add minced habanero chiles.

Yield: 8 cups

Approx Per Cup: Cal 133; Prot 1 g; Carbo 31 g; T Fat <1 g; 1% Calories from Fat; Chol 0 mg; Fiber 1 g; Sod 9 mg

■

Of the half million cancer deaths in the United States each year, one-third are related to dietary factors. Eating more servings of fruits and vegetables lowers the risk of lung, colon and rectum, stomach, esophagus, oral cavity, and larynx cancer.

ORANGEY CARROT FENNEL SOUP

■

INGREDIENTS

1¹/₄ cups chopped onions
3¹/₂ cups thinly sliced carrots
4 cups water
³/₄ cup unsweetened orange juice
1 teaspoon chicken bouillon granules
¹/₂ teaspoon grated orange zest
¹/₄ teaspoon fennel seeds, crushed
¹/₈ to ¹/₄ teaspoon white pepper

METHOD

■ Spray a heavy saucepan with nonstick cooking spray. Heat over medium heat until hot. Add the onions. Sauté until tender. Add the carrots and 2 tablespoons of the water and mix well.

■ Cook, covered, for 20 minutes or until the carrots are tender, stirring occasionally. Stir in the remaining water, orange juice, bouillon granules, orange zest, fennel seeds and white pepper. Bring to a boil; reduce heat.

■ Simmer for 8 minutes, stirring occasionally. Process the carrot mixture in several batches in a blender until puréed. Return the soup to the saucepan. Cook just until heated through, stirring frequently. Ladle into soup bowls.

Yield: 6 (1-cup) servings

Approx Per Serving: Cal 59; Prot 1 g; Carbo 14 g; T Fat <1 g; 4% Calories from Fat; Chol <1 mg; Fiber 3 g; Sod 218 mg

■

While all vegetables and fruits are healthy choices, try to include those that are nutrient-dense and offer the most cancer-protective compounds to your diet. Enjoy these with your other favorites: Dark green leafy and deep orange veggies pack the highest nutrition punch. Try greens like collard greens, spinach, kale and Swiss chard, along with red peppers, pumpkin, carrots, broccoli, and okra. Melons and citrus fruits are among those that get high marks for nutrition. Try papaya, cantaloupe, strawberries, oranges, tangerines, kiwi, mango, apricot, and watermelon. Although juice can count towards your "five or more" a day, experts recommend that most of your vegetable and fruit servings come from whole foods.[2]

MINTED CARROT AND ORANGE SOUP

■

INGREDIENTS

2	medium onions, finely chopped	2	tablespoons flour
1	tablespoon margarine	1	garlic clove, finely minced
5¹/₂	cups sliced carrots	1	teaspoon chopped shallot
3	cups chicken broth	¹/₂	cup loosely packed fresh mint leaves
¹/₄	teaspoon ground cloves	2	cups orange juice
¹/₄	teaspoon white pepper	■	Juice of ¹/₂ lemon

METHOD

■ Sauté the onions in the margarine in a saucepan until tender. Stir in the carrots, broth, cloves and white pepper. Simmer, covered, over medium heat for 10 to 15 minutes or until the carrots are tender, stirring occasionally.

■ Stir the flour into ¹/₃ cup of the soup stock. Stir the flour mixture into the soup. Simmer for 5 minutes or until thickened, stirring constantly. Remove from heat. Let stand for 15 to 20 minutes. Stir in the garlic, shallot and mint.

■ Process the soup mixture in several batches in a blender until puréed. Combine with the orange juice and lemon juice in a bowl and mix well. Chill, covered, until serving time.

■ Ladle the soup into chilled soup bowls. Garnish with orange slices and/or sprigs of fresh mint.

Yield: 8 servings

Approx Per Serving: Cal 112; Prot 4 g; Carbo 20 g; T Fat 2 g; 18% Calories from Fat; Chol 0 mg; Fiber 3 g; Sod 339 mg

CHICKEN VEGETABLE SOUP

INGREDIENTS

14	cups water	1 1/2	teaspoons whole thyme
3	pounds chicken breasts, skinned	3	garlic cloves, minced
1	large onion, cut into quarters	1	tablespoon vegetable oil
2	ribs celery, cut into quarters	1/2	cup pearl barley
1	tablespoon black peppercorns	2	(14-ounce) cans whole tomatoes, coarsely chopped
2	bay leaves	5	cups tightly packed torn fresh spinach
2	garlic cloves, cut into halves	1/4	teaspoon salt
1/2	cup sliced carrot	1/4	teaspoon pepper
1/2	cup sliced celery		
1/2	cup sliced parsnip		
1/2	cup chopped onion		

METHOD

■ Combine the water, chicken, 1 onion, 2 ribs celery, peppercorns, bay leaves and 2 garlic cloves in a stockpot. Bring to a boil; reduce heat.

■ Cook over medium heat for 1 hour. Remove the chicken with a slotted spoon to a bowl. Chill, covered, for 15 minutes. Chop the chicken into bite-size pieces, reserving the bones. Chill the chicken, covered, in the refrigerator.

■ Add the bones to the stockpot. Simmer for 1 hour, stirring occasionally. Strain the stock through a sieve into a bowl, discarding the solids.

■ Sauté the carrot, 1/2 cup celery, parsnip, 1/2 cup onion, thyme and garlic in the oil in a skillet over medium heat for 2 minutes. Add the barley and mix well. Sauté for 1 minute. Stir in the reserved stock and undrained tomatoes and mix well.

■ Bring to a boil; reduce heat. Simmer, covered, for 1 hour, stirring occasionally. Stir in the chicken, spinach, salt and pepper. Cook for 1 minute or until the spinach wilts. Ladle into soup bowls.

Yield: 11 (1 1/2-cup) servings

Approx Per Serving: Cal 180; Prot 22 g; Carbo 15 g; T Fat 4 g; 18% Calories from Fat; Chol 51 mg; Fiber 4 g; Sod 230 mg

Hot-and-Sour Soup

From Lahey Clinic Executive Chef John R. Di Sessa, C.E.C.

■

INGREDIENTS

2	tablespoons chopped scallion or cilantro	1	pound tofu, chopped
1	tablespoon minced gingerroot	1/4	cup white vinegar
8	ounces pork butt, shredded	■	Black soy sauce to taste
8	ounces Chinese cabbage, shredded	■	Salt to taste
4	ounces bamboo shoots, shredded	■	Black and white pepper to taste
3	tablespoons black fungus, soaked, tied, chopped	2	ounces cornstarch
3	tablespoons tiger lily buds, soaked, tied in a knot	2	eggs, lightly beaten
		2	tablespoons sesame oil
		3	ounces scallions
3	quarts chicken stock	1	ounce cilantro leaves

METHOD

■ Heat a large nonstick saucepan sprayed with nonstick cooking spray until hot. Stir-fry 2 tablespoons scallions and gingerroot in the hot skillet. Add the pork.

■ Stir-fry until the pork is cooked through. Stir in the cabbage, bamboo shoots, black fungus and tiger lily buds. Stir-fry until the cabbage is tender-crisp.

■ Reserve 2 cups of the stock. Add the remaining stock and tofu to the pork mixture and mix well. Bring to a simmer, stirring occasionally. Stir in the vinegar, soy sauce, salt, black pepper and white pepper. Add a mixture of the reserved stock and cornstarch and mix well.

■ Cook until thickened, stirring constantly. Add a small amount of the hot soup to the eggs. Add the eggs to the hot soup gradually, stirring constantly. Bring to a simmer, stirring occasionally. Stir in the sesame oil. Ladle into soup bowls. Top with 3 ounces scallions and cilantro leaves.

Yield: 16 (1-cup) servings

Approx Per Serving: Cal 111; Prot 8 g; Carbo 9 g; T Fat 5 g; 40% Calories from Fat; Chol 41 mg; Fiber 1 g; Sod 540 mg

Rainbow Vegetable Orzo Soup

Ingredients

1	cup dried lentils	$1/2$	teaspoon whole basil
4	cups water	$1/2$	teaspoon whole marjoram
3	(10-ounce) cans reduced-sodium chicken broth	$1/2$	teaspoon whole oregano
1	(28-ounce) can whole tomatoes	$1/2$	teaspoon whole thyme
1	(16-ounce) package frozen Italian green beans	$1/2$	teaspoon pepper
1	(6-ounce) can tomato paste	3	garlic cloves, minced
$1^{1}/2$	cups chopped onions	1	bay leaf
1	cup sliced carrot	2	cups water
1	cup chopped celery	1	cup orzo
$1/2$	cup chopped red bell pepper	$1/4$	cup white wine vinegar
1	tablespoon brown sugar	1	cup plus 1 tablespoon seasoned croutons

Method

- Sort and rinse the lentils. Combine the lentils, 4 cups water, broth, undrained tomatoes, green beans, tomato paste, onions, carrot, celery, red pepper, brown sugar, basil, marjoram, oregano, thyme, pepper, garlic and bay leaf in a stockpot and mix well. Bring to a boil; reduce heat.
- Simmer, covered, for 30 minutes, stirring occasionally. Add 2 cups water, orzo and wine vinegar and mix well.
- Simmer, covered, for 30 minutes longer or until the lentils are tender, stirring occasionally. Discard the bay leaf. Ladle into soup bowls. Sprinkle with the seasoned croutons.

Yield: 14 (1-cup) servings

Approx Per Serving: Cal 161; Prot 8 g; Carbo 30 g; T Fat 2 g; 9% Calories from Fat; Chol 1 mg; Fiber 6 g; Sod 267 mg

WILD MUSHROOM SOUP

■

INGREDIENTS

2	pounds assorted wild mushrooms
3	shallots, minced
2	sprigs of fresh thyme
1/2	bay leaf
3	cups skim milk
■	Salt and pepper to taste
1	teaspoon cornstarch

METHOD

■ Chop the mushrooms, reserving 8 ounces. Sauté the remaining mushrooms, shallots, thyme and bay leaf in a saucepan sprayed with nonstick cooking spray for 5 minutes. Stir in the skim milk.

■ Simmer for 10 minutes, stirring frequently. Strain, discarding the solids. Return to the saucepan.

■ Season with salt and pepper. Stir in a mixture of the cornstarch and a small amount of water. Cook until thickened, stirring constantly.

■ Sauté the reserved mushrooms in a nonstick skillet sprayed with nonstick cooking spray until tender; drain. Ladle the soup into soup bowls. Sprinkle with the sautéed mushrooms. Serve immediately.

Yield: 8 (1-cup) servings

Approx Per Serving: Cal 64; Prot 7 g; Carbo 10 g; T Fat <1 g; 2% Calories from Fat; Chol 2 mg; Fiber 1 g; Sod 48 mg

MICROWAVE POTATO CHOWDER

INGREDIENTS

1 tablespoon margarine	2 bay leaves
1 cup chopped green onions	1 cup skim milk
1/2 cup chopped red bell pepper	1 cup frozen whole kernel corn, thawed, drained
1/2 cup chopped green bell pepper	1/4 cup chopped fresh parsley
2 pounds potatoes, coarsely chopped	1/8 teaspoon cayenne pepper
3 cups chicken broth	Salt and black pepper to taste
2 teaspoons thyme	

METHOD

- Place the margarine in a microwave-safe dish. Microwave on High for 45 to 60 seconds or until melted. Stir in the green onions and bell peppers.
- Microwave on High for 3 minutes. Add the potatoes, broth, thyme and bay leaves. Microwave on High for 20 minutes or until the potatoes are tender, stirring twice. Discard the bay leaves.
- Remove 4 cups of the potatoes with a slotted spoon to a blender container. Add the skim milk. Process until puréed. Return the puréed potato mixture to the remaining potato mixture.
- Stir in the corn, parsley, cayenne pepper, salt and black pepper. Microwave on High for 3 minutes; stir. Ladle into soup bowls.

Yield: 6 servings

Approx Per Serving: Cal 228; Prot 8 g; Carbo 44 g; T Fat 3 g; 12% Calories from Fat; Chol 1 mg; Fiber 4 g; Sod 444 mg

Pumpkin Soup with Pheasant Breast and Fried Ginger

From Lahey Clinic Executive Chef John R. Di Sessa, C.E.C.

■

Ingredients

1	small pumpkin, cut into halves, seeded	1/2	cup canola oil, at room temperature
3	tablespoons olive oil	2	pheasant breasts, skinned
■	Salt and pepper to taste	1	tablespoon canola oil
8	sprigs of fresh thyme	1/4	cup chopped dried cranberries, rehydrated
1/4	cup chopped preserved ginger	1/4	cup pepitas
2	cups chicken stock	4	sprigs of fresh thyme
3	tablespoons butter	■	Freshly ground pepper to taste
1/2	cup julienned fresh gingerroot	4	teaspoons pumpkin seed oil

Method

■ Rub the pumpkin with the olive oil and season with salt and pepper. Arrange the pumpkin halves cut side down in a baking pan. Place 4 sprigs of thyme under each pumpkin half.

■ Add enough water to the baking pan to measure 1/2 inch. Roast at 350 degrees for 45 to 60 minutes or until the pumpkin is tender. Cool slightly.

■ Spoon the pumpkin pulp into a blender container. Add the undrained preserved ginger and stock. Process until puréed. Season with salt and pepper. Spoon into a saucepan. Cook over medium heat for 5 minutes or until heated through, stirring frequently. Whisk in the butter. Adjust the seasonings.

■ Combine the julienned gingerroot and 1/2 cup canola oil in a saucepan. Cook over medium heat for 8 to 10 minutes or until brown and crispy; drain.

■ Season the pheasant with salt and pepper. Heat 1 tablespoon canola oil in a skillet over medium heat until hot. Add the pheasant. Cook for 5 to 7 minutes or until a meat thermometer registers 165 degrees. Remove from heat. Let stand for 3 minutes. Cut into thin slices. Season with salt and pepper.

■ Ladle the soup into 4 shallow soup bowls. Arrange the sliced pheasant in the center. Sprinkle with the cranberries, pepitas, fried ginger and 4 sprigs of thyme. Top with pepper. Drizzle 1 teaspoon pumpkin seed oil around the edge of each bowl.

Yield: 4 servings

Approx Per Serving: Cal 712; Prot 49 g; Carbo 41 g; T Fat 40 g; 50% Calories from Fat; Chol 129 mg; Fiber 5 g; Sod 501 mg
One tablespoon of oil per serving is absorbed in the cooking process.

TORTILLA SOUP

■

INGREDIENTS

2   (6-inch) corn tortillas, cut into strips
1   teaspoon olive oil
¹/₂   cup chopped onion
1   teaspoon chopped garlic
8   ounces plum tomatoes, coarsely chopped
1   tablespoon chopped green chiles
1   tablespoon dark chili powder
■   Oregano to taste
8   cups chicken broth
¹/₄   cup chopped fresh cilantro
1   cup plain reduced-fat yogurt

METHOD

■ Arrange the tortilla strips on a nonstick baking sheet. Spray lightly with nonstick cooking spray. Bake at 375 degrees until brown and crispy.

■ Heat the olive oil in a medium saucepan over medium heat until hot. Add the onion and garlic. Cook, covered, for 10 minutes or until the onion is tender, stirring occasionally. Add the tomatoes, chiles, chili powder and oregano and mix well.

■ Cook for 5 minutes or until the tomatoes begin to soften, stirring occasionally. Stir in the broth. Simmer, covered, for 40 minutes or until the vegetables are tender, stirring occasionally.

■ Process the soup in batches in a blender until puréed. Return the purée to the saucepan. Cook just until heated through, stirring frequently. Ladle into soup bowls. Top each serving with an equal amount of the tortilla strips, cilantro and yogurt.

Yield: 6 (1¹/₂-cup) servings

Approx Per Serving: Cal 123; Prot 10 g; Carbo 12 g; T Fat 4 g; 28% Calories from Fat; Chol 2 mg; Fiber 2 g; Sod 1095 mg

■

Skim fat from home made soups and gravies by chilling and removing the fat layer that rises to the surface. For low fat gravy or sauce: Mix thoroughly 1 tablespoon cornstarch or arrowroot or 2 tablespoons flour with 1 cup of cold fat-free liquid. Add to skimmed drippings or broth. Cook until thickened or of the desired consistency.[5]

VEGETABLE SOUP

■

INGREDIENTS

3/4 cup chopped onion
3/4 cup chopped green bell pepper
3/4 cup chopped celery
2   garlic cloves, minced
1   tablespoon canola oil
1 1/2 cups chopped fresh tomatoes
1   (12-ounce) can beer
1   cup drained canned kidney beans, rinsed
2   tablespoons wine vinegar

1   tablespoon chopped jalapeño chile
1   tablespoon chili powder
1   teaspoon oregano
1   teaspoon cumin
1/2 teaspoon allspice
1/2 teaspoon cayenne pepper
1/4 cup shredded reduced-fat Cheddar cheese
1/4 cup shredded reduced-fat Monterey Jack cheese

METHOD

■ Sauté the onion, green pepper, celery and garlic in the canola oil in a large saucepan for 5 minutes or until tender. Stir in the tomatoes. Simmer for 10 minutes, stirring occasionally. Add the beer, beans, wine vinegar, chile, chili powder, oregano, cumin, allspice and cayenne pepper and mix well.

■ Simmer for 15 to 20 minutes longer or until of the desired consistency, stirring occasionally. Ladle into soup bowls. Sprinkle with equal amounts of a mixture of the Cheddar cheese and Monterey Jack cheese.

Yield: 4 servings

Approx Per Serving: Cal 229; Prot 11 g; Carbo 27 g; T Fat 7 g; 27% Calories from Fat; Chol 8 mg; Fiber 9 g; Sod 141 mg

CREAM OF VEGETABLE SOUP

**From the recipe files of Dr. Sara M. Jordan.
Modified by Lahey Clinic Executive Chef
John R. Di Sessa, C.E.C.**

■

INGREDIENTS

1/4 cup minced onion
1/4 cup minced celery
1/4 cup minced carrot
1/4 cup minced leek
2   cups vegetable broth
2   cups skim milk
3   tablespoons cornstarch
■   Salt and white pepper to taste
2   tablespoons finely chopped spinach
4   slices French bread, toasted

METHOD

■ Coat a heavy saucepan with nonstick cooking spray. Heat until hot. Add the onion, celery, carrot and leek. Sauté until the onion is tender. Stir in the broth and skim milk.

■ Bring to a boil, stirring frequently. Add a mixture of the cornstarch and a small amount of water to form a paste. Add the paste to the boiling liquid gradually, stirring constantly. Cook until thickened and smooth, stirring constantly; skim off the top as needed. Continue cooking until the carrot is tender. Season with salt and white pepper.

■ Process the soup in a blender or food processor until smooth. Fold in the spinach. Place 1 slice of French bread in each of 4 soup bowls. Ladle the soup over the bread. Serve immediately.

Yield: 4 servings

Approx Per Serving: Cal 165; Prot 8 g; Carbo 31 g; T Fat 2 g; 8% Calories from Fat; Chol 2 mg; Fiber 2 g; Sod 728 mg

■

Use puréed cooked vegetables such as carrots, potatoes, or cauliflower to thicken soups and sauces, instead of cream, egg yolks, and butter. Soft tofu is also a good thickening agent.[5]

Very Veggie Barley Soup

Ingredients

1 cup chopped onion	1/4 teaspoon pepper
1/2 cup chopped celery	1/4 teaspoon whole oregano
2 tablespoons chopped fresh parsley	1/4 teaspoon whole basil
1 garlic clove, minced	1/4 teaspoon whole thyme
7 cups water	1/4 teaspoon curry powder
1 (28-ounce) can chopped whole tomatoes	1 bay leaf
1 cup thinly sliced carrot	1 cup thinly sliced leeks
1/2 cup barley	1 cup shredded cabbage
1 tablespoon beef bouillon granules	1/2 cup chopped peeled turnip

Method

■ Coat a large heavy saucepan with nonstick cooking spray. Heat over medium heat until hot. Add the onion, celery, parsley and garlic. Sauté until the vegetables are tender.

■ Add the water, undrained tomatoes, carrot, barley, bouillon granules, pepper, oregano, basil, thyme, curry powder and bay leaf and mix well. Bring to a boil; reduce heat.

■ Simmer, covered, for 20 minutes, stirring occasionally. Add the leeks, cabbage and turnip and mix well. Simmer, covered, for 15 minutes longer, stirring occasionally. Discard the bay leaf. Ladle into soup bowls.

Yield: 12 (1-cup) servings

Approx Per Serving: Cal 62; Prot 2 g; Carbo 14 g; T Fat <1 g; 4% Calories from Fat; Chol <1 mg; Fiber 3 g; Sod 330 mg

Chilled Yellow Pepper and White Bean Soup

From Lahey Clinic Executive Chef John R. Di Sessa, C.E.C.

■

INGREDIENTS

3	yellow, orange or red bell peppers
1	tablespoon olive oil
1	white onion, chopped
$^1/_8$	teaspoon crushed red pepper
3	cups reduced-sodium chicken broth
1	(16-ounce) can cannellini beans, drained, rinsed
	Salt and pepper to taste
1	bunch arugula, sliced

METHOD

■ Char the bell peppers over a gas flame until the skin is blackened and blistered on all sides. Place the peppers in a nonrecycled paper bag immediately and seal tightly. Let stand for 10 minutes. Peel, seed and chop the bell peppers.

■ Heat the olive oil in a heavy saucepan over medium-high heat until hot. Add the onion. Sauté for 5 minutes or until tender. Stir in the bell peppers and crushed red pepper.

■ Sauté for 1 minute. Stir in the broth and beans. Bring to a boil; reduce heat. Simmer, covered, for 15 minutes.

■ Strain the soup, reserving the liquid. Process the vegetable mixture in a food processor until puréed. Add 2 cups of the reserved liquid gradually, processing constantly just until blended. Transfer the mixture to a bowl. Stir in the remaining reserved liquid. Season with salt and pepper.

■ Chill, covered, until serving time. Ladle the soup into soup bowls. Top with the arugula. May be prepared 1 day in advance and stored, covered, in the refrigerator.

Yield: 4 servings

Approx Per Serving: Cal 172; Prot 8 g; Carbo 24 g; T Fat 5 g; 27% Calories from Fat; Chol 3 mg; Fiber 6 g; Sod 320 mg

■

Canned, processed, and frozen convenience foods tend to be high in sodium. If you are limiting your sodium intake, read the labels of these foods carefully.[5]

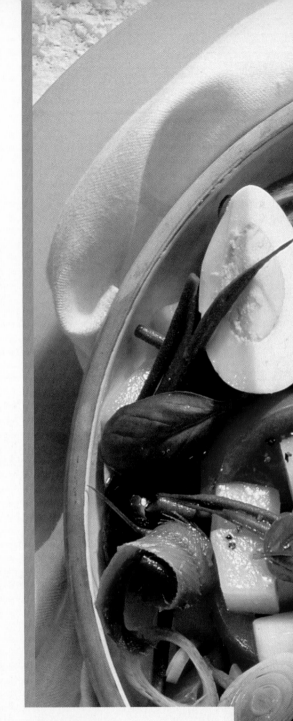

SALADS, SIDES & BREADS

CANTALOUPE BLUEBERRY SALAD

■

INGREDIENTS

1   cup reduced-fat yogurt
1   tablespoon lemon juice
1½ teaspoons poppy seeds
1   teaspoon grated orange zest
1   medium cantaloupe, peeled, seeded
24 leaves Boston lettuce
2   cups fresh blueberries

METHOD

■ Combine the yogurt, lemon juice, poppy seeds and
orange zest in a bowl and mix well. Chill, covered, in
the refrigerator.
■ Cut the cantaloupe lengthwise into 32 slices. Arrange
4 slices on each of 8 lettuce-lined salad plates. Sprinkle
each salad with ¼ cup of the blueberries. Spoon the yogurt
mixture over the top.

Yield: 8 servings

*Approx Per Serving: Cal 67; Prot 3 g; Carbo 14 g; T Fat 1 g;
10% Calories from Fat; Chol 2 mg; Fiber 2 g; Sod 31 mg*

CALIFORNIA FRUIT SALAD WITH POPPY SEED DRESSING

INGREDIENTS

1   (20-ounce) can pineapple chunks, drained
1   (11-ounce) can mandarin oranges, drained
1   Red Delicious apple, chopped

1   banana, sliced
1   avocado, chopped
1/4   cup raisins
    Poppy Seed Dressing

METHOD

- Combine the pineapple, mandarin oranges, apple, banana, avocado and raisins in a bowl and mix gently. Add the Poppy Seed Dressing and toss gently to coat.
- Chill, covered, for 2 hours or until serving time.

POPPY SEED DRESSING

INGREDIENTS

1/3   cup honey
1/4   cup orange juice
1/4   cup canola oil
2   teaspoons poppy seeds

1/2   teaspoon lemon juice
1/4   teaspoon salt
1/4   teaspoon prepared mustard

METHOD

- Combine the honey, orange juice, canola oil, poppy seeds, lemon juice, salt and prepared mustard in a jar with a tight-fitting lid and seal tightly.
- Shake until mixed. Store in the refrigerator.

Yield: 8 servings

Approx Per Serving: Cal 245; Prot 1 g; Carbo 40 g; T Fat 11 g; 37% Calories from Fat; Chol 0 mg; Fiber 3 g; Sod 80 mg

CHICKEN SALAD WITH GRAPES AND APPLES

INGREDIENTS

1	pound boneless skinless chicken breasts, cooked, chopped
1½	cups seedless red grapes
1	cup chopped unpeeled Red Delicious apple
⅔	cup chopped celery
¼	cup golden raisins
2	tablespoons chopped red onion
¼	cup plain nonfat yogurt
3	tablespoons reduced-fat mayonnaise
1½	tablespoons fresh lemon juice
1	tablespoon chopped fresh celery leaves
¼	teaspoon salt
6	leaves Boston lettuce

METHOD

■ Combine the chicken, grapes, apple, celery, raisins and red onion in a bowl and toss gently. Combine the yogurt, mayonnaise, lemon juice, celery leaves and salt in a bowl and mix well. Add to the chicken mixture and toss to coat.

■ Chill, covered, until serving time. Spoon onto each of 6 lettuce-lined salad plates.

Yield: 6 (1-cup) servings

Approx Per Serving: Cal 173; Prot 16 g; Carbo 18 g; T Fat 5 g; 23% Calories from Fat; Chol 44 mg; Fiber 2 g; Sod 205 mg

CURRIED CHICKEN SALAD

INGREDIENTS

1/2 cup nonfat yogurt

1/2 cup reduced-fat sour cream

1 tablespoon reduced-fat mayonnaise

2 teaspoons curry powder

1/4 teaspoon pepper

1/4 teaspoon salt

4 drops of hot pepper sauce

2 garlic cloves, minced

12 ounces boneless skinless chicken breasts, cooked, chopped

1 (8-ounce) can unsweetened pineapple tidbits, drained

1/2 cup sliced celery

1/3 cup minced green onions

1/4 cup minced radishes

2 tablespoons slivered almonds, toasted

6 leaves Boston lettuce

METHOD

■ Combine the yogurt and sour cream in a bowl. Stir in the mayonnaise, curry powder, pepper, salt, hot pepper sauce and garlic. Stir in the chicken, pineapple, celery, green onions, radishes and almonds.

■ Chill, covered, in the refrigerator. Spoon onto each of 3 lettuce-lined salad plates just before serving.

■ You may substitute 1 cup fromage blanc for the yogurt and sour cream.

Yield: 3 (1-cup) servings

Approx Per Serving: Cal 298; Prot 29 g; Carbo 22 g; T Fat 11 g; 32% Calories from Fat; Chol 78 mg; Fiber 2 g; Sod 356 mg

SEAFOOD SALAD

■

INGREDIENTS

20	ounces snapper fillets	3/4	teaspoon salt
1	tablespoon olive oil	1	cup minced red onion
1/2	cup fresh lemon juice	6	green onions, minced
1/2	cup fresh orange juice	1	tablespoon minced garlic
1/4	cup fresh lime juice	1/2	cup minced parsley
2	tablespoons olive oil	1/4	teaspoon freshly ground pepper
1	tablespoon white wine vinegar	■	Lettuce leaves

METHOD

■ Arrange the snapper on a nonstick baking sheet sprayed with nonstick cooking spray. Brush with 1 tablespoon olive oil. Bake at 400 degrees for 15 minutes or until the fish flakes easily. Flake the fish into a bowl.

■ Whisk the lemon juice, orange juice, lime juice, 2 tablespoons olive oil, wine vinegar, salt, red onion, green onions, garlic, parsley and pepper in a bowl. Pour over the fish and toss gently to coat. Spoon onto each of 6 lettuce-lined salad plates.

Yield: 6 servings

Approx Per Serving: Cal 155; Prot 14 g; Carbo 8 g; T Fat 8 g; 44% Calories from Fat; Chol 23 mg; Fiber 1 g; Sod 325 mg

Tuna Bean Salad

■

Ingredients

1   (15-ounce) can cannellini beans, drained, rinsed
1   (12-ounce) can water-pack white tuna, drained, flaked
1   large tomato, seeded, chopped
1/4 cup finely chopped onion
1   to 2 tablespoons fresh lemon juice
2   teaspoons Dijon mustard
1/4 cup olive oil
1/4 cup chopped fresh basil
■   Salt and freshly ground pepper to taste
■   Lettuce leaves

Method

■ Combine the beans, tuna, tomato and onion in a bowl and mix gently. Whisk the lemon juice and Dijon mustard in a bowl. Add the olive oil gradually, whisking constantly until blended.

■ Pour the dressing over the bean mixture and toss gently to coat. Stir in the chopped basil. Season with salt and pepper.

■ Spoon the salad onto each of 6 lettuce-lined salad plates. Garnish with fresh basil leaves.

Yield: 6 (1-cup) servings

Approx Per Serving: Cal 213; Prot 18 g; Carbo 13 g; T Fat 10 g; 43% Calories from Fat; Chol 17 mg; Fiber 3 g; Sod 384 mg

■

Omega-3 fatty acids— polyunsaturated fatty acids of a somewhat different structure—are found mostly in seafood, especially higher-fat, cold-water varieties, such as mackerel, albacore tuna, salmon, sardines, and lake trout. Both soybean oil and canola oil supply some omega-3s, too. Although inconclusive, some research suggests that omega-3s may help prevent blood platelets from clotting and sticking to artery walls. As a result, they may help lower the risk for blocked blood vessels and heart attacks. Omega-3s may help prevent arteries from hardening.[4]

Black Bean Salad

From Lahey Clinic Executive Chef John R. Di Sessa, C.E.C.

Serve as an accompaniment to grilled fish, shellfish, poultry, game, or other meats.

Ingredients

1 1/2 pounds dried black beans
14 ounces red, green and/or yellow bell peppers, chopped
1 1/2 ounces red onion, chopped
1 1/2 jalapeño chiles, minced
3/4 ounce minced garlic
Cilantro leaves to taste
3/4 cup plus 2 tablespoons Lime Cilantro Vinaigrette (page 73)

Method

Sort and rinse the beans. Combine the beans with enough water to cover in a bowl. Let stand for 8 to 10 hours; drain. Combine the beans with additional water in a stockpot. Cook until tender; drain.

Combine the beans, bell peppers, red onion, chiles, garlic and cilantro in a bowl and mix gently. Add the Lime Cilantro Vinaigrette and toss to coat. Marinate, covered, in the refrigerator for several hours to allow the flavors to marry.

Yield: 10 servings

Approx Per Serving: Cal 275; Prot 15 g; Carbo 42 g; T Fat 6 g; 18% Calories from Fat; Chol 0 mg; Fiber 15 g; Sod 53 mg

Corn and Black Bean Salad

From Lahey Clinic Executive Chef John R. Di Sessa, C.E.C.

■

Ingredients

2   (16-ounce) cans black beans, drained, rinsed
2   cups whole kernel corn
1/4   cup chopped fresh cilantro
1/4   cup chopped green bell pepper
1/4   cup chopped red bell pepper
2   tablespoons minced red onion

2   tablespoons extra-virgin olive oil
1   teaspoon lemon juice
1   teaspoon honey
1   teaspoon minced garlic
■   Salt and pepper to taste
■   Lettuce leaves, chilled

Method

■ Combine the beans, corn, cilantro, green pepper, red pepper and red onion in a bowl and mix gently. Whisk the olive oil, lemon juice, honey and garlic in a bowl. Pour over the bean mixture and toss to mix.

■ Let stand at room temperature for 30 minutes. Season with salt and pepper. Spoon onto each of 8 salad plates lined with chilled lettuce leaves.

Yield: 8 servings

Approx Per Serving: Cal 157; Prot 7 g; Carbo 24 g; T Fat 5 g; 25% Calories from Fat; Chol 0 mg; Fiber 7 g; Sod 355 mg

Barley, Corn and Roasted Red Pepper Salad

Ingredients

1 1/2 cups pearl barley
8 cups cold water
2 teaspoons salt
1/2 cup reduced-fat mayonnaise
2/3 cup grated Parmesan cheese
2 tablespoons red wine vinegar
2 cups fresh whole kernel corn
1 (7-ounce) jar roasted red peppers, drained, cut into 1/2-inch pieces
2/3 cup thinly sliced green onions or scallions
■ Salt and pepper to taste

Method

■ Rinse the barley in a colander with cold water. Combine the barley, 8 cups cold water and 2 teaspoons salt in a saucepan. Bring to a boil; reduce heat.

■ Cook, partially covered, over medium-low heat for 30 minutes or just until the barley is tender, stirring occasionally; drain.

■ Whisk the mayonnaise in a bowl. Stir in the cheese and wine vinegar. Combine the barley, corn, red peppers and 1/2 cup of the green onions in a large bowl and mix gently. Add the mayonnaise mixture and toss to coat. Season with salt and pepper to taste. Spoon into a serving bowl. Sprinkle with the remaining green onions.

Yield: 8 servings

Approx Per Serving: Cal 260; Prot 9 g; Carbo 40 g; T Fat 9 g; 28% Calories from Fat; Chol 12 mg; Fiber 7 g; Sod 943 mg

Barley, Corn and Roasted Red Pepper Salad

65

Caesar Salad

∎

INGREDIENTS

4 (1-ounce) slices French bread	∎ Caesar Salad Dressing
8 cups torn romaine	

METHOD

∎ Cut the bread into ³/₄-inch cubes. Arrange the cubes on a nonstick baking sheet. Toast at 300 degrees for 15 minutes or until brown and crispy, stirring occasionally.

∎ Combine the croutons and lettuce in a salad bowl. Add the Caesar Salad Dressing and toss to coat. Serve immediately.

Yield: 4 servings

Approx Per Serving: Cal 139; Prot 7 g; Carbo 21 g; T Fat 3 g; 20% Calories from Fat; Chol 5 mg; Fiber 3 g; Sod 410 mg
Nutritional information includes the entire amount of dressing.

Caesar Salad Dressing

∎

INGREDIENTS

¹/₄ cup grated Parmesan cheese	¹/₂ teaspoon anchovy paste
¹/₄ cup nonfat mayonnaise	¹/₂ teaspoon Worcestershire sauce
¹/₄ cup water	¹/₄ teaspoon freshly ground pepper
2 tablespoons fresh lemon juice	¹/₈ teaspoon dry mustard
2 garlic cloves, minced	

METHOD

∎ Combine the cheese, mayonnaise, water and lemon juice in a bowl and mix well. Stir in the garlic, anchovy paste, Worcestershire sauce, pepper and dry mustard.

FRUITY SWEET POTATO SALAD

■

INGREDIENTS

2 cups chopped cooked sweet potatoes
1 apple, chopped
1 cup chopped celery
1 (11-ounce) can mandarin oranges, drained
1 (8-ounce) can juice-pack pineapple tidbits, drained
1/4 cup chopped pecans
1/4 cup reduced-fat sour cream
1/4 cup mayonnaise
2 tablespoons skim milk
1/2 teaspoon salt
■ Lettuce leaves

METHOD

■ Combine the sweet potatoes, apple, celery, mandarin oranges, pineapple and pecans in a bowl and mix gently.
■ Combine the sour cream, mayonnaise, skim milk and salt in a bowl and mix well. Add to the sweet potato mixture and toss to coat.
■ Chill, covered, until serving time. Spoon onto each of 8 lettuce-lined salad plates.

Yield: 8 servings

Approx Per Serving: Cal 169; Prot 2 g; Carbo 22 g; T Fat 9 g; 45% Calories from Fat; Chol 8 mg; Fiber 2 g; Sod 208 mg

■

For Mock Sour Cream, blend 1/2 cup plain nonfat yogurt, 1/2 cup nonfat cottage cheese, and 1 tablespoon lemon juice.[5]

Toast nuts to enhance flavor, thus cutting down on the amount needed in a recipe.[5]

FRUIT AND NUT WHEAT BERRY TABOULI

From Lahey Clinic Executive Chef John R. Di Sessa, C.E.C.

INGREDIENTS

1	quart water
1 1/3	cups white wheat berries
■	Sections of 2 seedless oranges, cut into halves
1/4	cup fresh lemon juice
1/2	cucumber, peeled, seeded, chopped
1 1/2	cups chopped flat-leaf parsley
1/2	cup chopped fresh mint
1/2	cup finely sliced scallions
1/4	cup chopped walnuts, toasted
1/4	cup golden raisins, chopped
1	garlic clove, minced
■	Salt and pepper to taste

METHOD

■ Combine the water and wheat berries in a 2-quart saucepan and cover tightly. Bring to a boil over medium heat; reduce heat. Simmer for 2 hours or until the wheat berries are tender but chewy, adding additional water as needed. Pour into a colander. Rinse with cold water; drain.

■ Combine the wheat berries and oranges in a bowl and toss gently. Stir in the lemon juice, cucumber, parsley, mint, scallions, walnuts, raisins and garlic. Season with salt and pepper. Chill, covered, for 1 hour or longer before serving.

Yield: 6 servings

Approx Per Serving: Cal 191; Prot 6 g; Carbo 38 g; T Fat 4 g; 16% Calories from Fat; Chol 0 mg; Fiber 8 g; Sod 17 mg

TABOULI

INGREDIENTS

1¼ cups bulgur
1¼ cups boiling water
1 pound tomatoes, chopped
1 cucumber, peeled, seeded, chopped
¾ cup chopped fresh parsley
½ yellow bell pepper, chopped

1 bunch green onions, sliced
2 tablespoons chopped fresh mint
½ teaspoon salt
⅓ cup lemon juice
2 tablespoons olive oil

METHOD

- Combine the bulgur and boiling water in a heatproof bowl and mix well. Let stand for 30 minutes or until the water is absorbed.
- Add the tomatoes, cucumber, parsley, yellow pepper, green onions, mint and salt and mix gently. Add a mixture of the lemon juice and olive oil and toss to mix. Serve immediately or chill, covered, until serving time.

Yield: 6 (1-cup) servings

Approx Per Serving: Cal 173; Prot 5 g; Carbo 30 g; T Fat 5 g; 25% Calories from Fat; Chol 0 mg; Fiber 7 g; Sod 213 mg

SEA VEGETABLE SALAD

∎

INGREDIENTS

2	cups dried wakame	2	tablespoons brown rice syrup
1	cup dried arame	1	tablespoon tamari
1/4	cup rice vinegar	1/2	teaspoon cayenne pepper
2	tablespoons toasted sesame oil	1/4	cup sesame seeds, toasted

METHOD

∎ Combine the wakame with enough warm water to cover in a bowl. Let stand for 15 minutes or until softened; drain. Cut crosswise into julienne strips. Combine the arame with enough warm water to cover in a bowl. Let stand for 15 minutes or until softened; drain. Combine the seaweed in a bowl and mix well.

∎ Whisk the rice vinegar, sesame oil, rice syrup, tamari and cayenne pepper in a bowl until mixed. Add to the seaweed mixture and toss to coat. Stir in the sesame seeds. Chill, covered, until serving time.

Yield: 4 (3/4-cup) servings

Nutritional information is not available for this recipe.

Firecracker Tomato Salad

From Lahey Clinic Executive Chef John R. Di Sessa, C.E.C.

■

Ingredients

3   beefsteak tomatoes, thickly sliced
5   Roma tomatoes, cut into quarters
3   Golden Jubilee tomatoes, cut into wedges
1/2 cup fresh basil leaves
■   Sea salt and pepper to taste
■   Olive oil (optional)

Method

■ Toss the tomatoes with the basil leaves in a salad bowl.
  Sprinkle with sea salt and pepper. Drizzle with olive oil.
■ Try different varieties of tomatoes, such as Golden Round,
  Tiger-Striped, Red Cherry and/or Yellow Pear.

Yield: 6 servings

*Approx Per Serving: Cal 62; Prot 4 g; Carbo 12 g; T Fat 1 g;
10% Calories from Fat; Chol 0 mg; Fiber 5 g; Sod 19 mg*

■

Keep the edible peels on vegetables such as potatoes, cucumbers, and summer squash to increase fiber consumption.[4]

CREAMY TOFU AND HERB DRESSING

From Lahey Clinic Executive Chef John R. Di Sessa, C.E.C.

INGREDIENTS

1 cup chopped fresh basil
1 cup chopped fresh cilantro
2 teaspoons chopped fresh oregano
2 teaspoons Dijon mustard
1 garlic clove
12 ounces silken tofu, chopped
1/3 cup fresh lime juice
3/4 cup extra-virgin olive oil
▪ Salt and freshly ground pepper to taste

METHOD

▪ Process the basil, cilantro, oregano, Dijon mustard and garlic in a blender or food processor until blended. Add the tofu and lime juice.

▪ Process until smooth. Add the olive oil in a fine stream, processing constantly until blended. Season with salt and pepper. For a thinner consistency, add a small amount of water or soy milk.

Yield: 12 (1/4-cup) servings

Approx Per Serving: Cal 142; Prot 2 g; Carbo 2 g; T Fat 14 g; 89% Calories from Fat; Chol 0 mg; Fiber <1 g; Sod 34 mg

Vinaigrette-Style Salad Dressing

From Lahey Clinic Executive Chef John R. Di Sessa, C.E.C.

■

The traditional oil to vinegar ratio for a classic vinaigrette is three parts to one part, respectively. In this recipe two-thirds of the oil is replaced by thickened stock. Using a thickened stock gives the new version excellent coating abilities. The texture is similar enough to that of the classic vinaigrette to effectively fool the mouth. Mixing the vinaigrette by using a regular or immersion blender not only adds to the dressing body; it also thoroughly distributes the oil.

INGREDIENTS

2	quarts vegetable stock	1	quart extra-virgin olive oil
1½	ounces arrowroot	1	tablespoon salt
1	quart red wine vinegar	■	Seasonings of choice (optional)

METHOD

■ Bring the stock to a boil in a large saucepan. Dissolve the arrowroot in a small amount of cold water in a bowl. Add to the stock gradually, stirring constantly. Cook until thick enough to lightly coat a spoon, stirring frequently. Let stand until cool.

■ Whip the wine vinegar and olive oil into the stock mixture. Add the salt and seasonings as desired. Store, covered, in the refrigerator.

■ Seasonings of choice may consist of prepared mustards, chopped fresh herbs, chopped drained capers, minced fresh vegetables, minced onions, minced garlic and minced citrus zest.

VARIATION

■ For Lime Cilantro Vinaigrette, add 1 bunch chopped fresh cilantro and the juice of 4 limes after adding the salt.

Yield: 64 (¼-cup) servings

Approx Per Serving: Cal 128; Prot <1 g; Carbo 1 g; T Fat 14 g; 97% Calories from Fat; Chol 0 mg; Fiber <1 g; Sod 144 mg

Roasted Fresh Asparagus

■

INGREDIENTS

1½ pounds fresh asparagus, trimmed

■ Salt and freshly ground pepper
to taste

2 teaspoons olive oil

1 teaspoon balsamic vinegar

METHOD

■ Toss the asparagus with the olive oil in a shallow roasting pan or baking sheet with sides. Season with salt and pepper. Arrange the asparagus in a single layer.

■ Roast at 450 degrees for 10 to 15 minutes or until tender and brown, shaking the pan once during the roasting process. Drizzle with the balsamic vinegar. Serve warm or at room temperature.

Yield: 4 servings

Approx Per Serving: Cal 61; Prot 4 g; Carbo 8 g; T Fat 3 g; 33% Calories from Fat; Chol 0 mg; Fiber 4 g; Sod 4 mg

Seasoned Asparagus

■

INGREDIENTS

1 pound fresh asparagus, trimmed

1 tablespoon olive oil

½ teaspoon chopped garlic

2 teaspoons balsamic vinegar

2 tablepoons orange juice

⅛ teaspoon chopped garlic

¼ cup slivered almonds, toasted

METHOD

■ Toss the asparagus with the olive oil in a baking pan. Arrange the asparagus in a single layer. Sprinkle with ½ teaspoon garlic.

■ Roast at 450 degrees for 8 to 10 minutes or until tender. Transfer the asparagus to a serving platter. Drizzle with a mixture of the balsamic vinegar, orange juice and ⅛ teaspoon garlic. Sprinkle with the almonds. Serve warm.

Yield: 4 servings

Approx Per Serving: Cal 113; Prot 4 g; Carbo 8 g; T Fat 8 g; 59% Calories from Fat; Chol 0 mg; Fiber 3 g; Sod 4 mg

Spicy Sour Cabbage

■

Ingredients

2	tablespoons soy sauce
2	tablespoons vinegar
2	tablespoons sugar
3	tablespoons vegetable oil
5	hot chiles
10	black peppercorns
1	(1-pound) head cabbage, shredded
1	green bell pepper, julienned
1	red bell pepper, julienned
1	tablespoon sesame oil

Method

■ Whisk the soy sauce, vinegar and sugar in a bowl. Heat the vegetable oil in a large skillet over high heat until hot. Add the chiles and peppercorns. Stir-fry for several seconds. Add the cabbage and bell peppers and mix well.

■ Stir-fry for 1 to 1½ minutes or until the vegetables are of the desired crispness. Stir in the soy sauce mixture. Stir-fry just until heated through. Discard the chiles and peppercorns.

■ Spoon the cabbage mixture into a serving bowl. Drizzle with the sesame oil. Serve hot or at room temperature.

Yield: 4 servings

Approx Per Serving: Cal 218; Prot 4 g; Carbo 23 g; T Fat 14 g; 55% Calories from Fat; Chol 0 mg; Fiber 5 g; Sod 500 mg

■

The Food Guide Pyramid recommends three to five servings of vegetables and two to four servings of fruit daily. Try to include at least one vitamin A-rich food, one vitamin C-rich food, and one high-fiber food in these selections. Eat vegetables from the cabbage family several times a week. Cruciferous vegetables, such as bok choy, broccoli, collards, cabbage, and turnips may help to protect against colon and rectal cancer.[4]

PINEAPPLE CARROT DELIGHT

INGREDIENTS

8	carrots, sliced	1	tablespoon (heaping) cornstarch
1	cup orange juice	1/2	teaspoon ginger
1	(16-ounce) can juice-pack pineapple tidbits	1/4	cup chopped fresh parsley

METHOD

■ Cook the carrots and orange juice in a saucepan until the carrots are tender-crisp. Drain the pineapple, reserving the juice. Mix the reserved juice, cornstarch and ginger in a bowl. Stir into the carrot mixture. Add the pineapple and mix gently.

■ Cook over low heat until thickened, stirring frequently. Sprinkle with the parsley.

Yield: 8 servings

Approx Per Serving: Cal 83; Prot 1 g; Carbo 20 g; T Fat <1 g; 3% Calories from Fat; Chol 0 mg; Fiber 3 g; Sod 27 mg

HERBED CORN ON THE COB

From Lahey Clinic Executive Chef John R. Di Sessa, C.E.C.

INGREDIENTS

4	ears of fresh corn	1	tablespoon water
1	tablespoon whole dillweed	1	teaspoon vegetable oil
1	teaspoon whole thyme	1	garlic clove, minced

METHOD

■ Remove the husks and silk from the corn. Mix the remaining ingredients in a bowl.

■ Rub the herb mixture evenly over the corn. Wrap each ear of corn in a piece of heavy-duty foil, twisting the ends to seal. Grill over medium-hot coals for 15 to 20 minutes or until the corn is tender, turning every 5 minutes.

Yield: 4 servings

Approx Per Serving: Cal 89; Prot 3 g; Carbo 17 g; T Fat 2 g; 20% Calories from Fat; Chol 0 mg; Fiber 2 g; Sod 14 mg

Spicy New Potatoes

■

Ingredients

2	pounds unpeeled new potatoes, cut into quarters
1 1/2	tablespoons olive oil
1	tablespoon margarine
3	tablespoons fresh lime juice
2	garlic cloves, minced
1	teaspoon coriander seeds, crushed
4	or 5 green onions with tops, chopped
1/2	cup chopped fresh flat-leaf parsley or cilantro
1 1/2	teaspoons chili powder
■	Salt and freshly ground pepper to taste
1/4	cup shredded Parmesan cheese

Method

■ Combine the potatoes with enough water to cover in a saucepan. Bring to a boil; reduce heat. Cook until tender-crisp; drain.

■ Heat the olive oil and margarine in a saucepan until the margarine melts. Stir in the lime juice, garlic and coriander seeds. Cook for 1 minute, stirring frequently.

■ Combine the potatoes with the margarine mixture in a bowl and toss gently. Add the green onions, parsley, chili powder, salt and pepper and mix gently. Sprinkle with the cheese. Serve hot or at room temperature.

Yield: 8 servings

Approx Per Serving: Cal 181; Prot 4 g; Carbo 31 g; T Fat 5 g; 25% Calories from Fat; Chol 2 mg; Fiber 3 g; Sod 92 mg

■

One vegetable group serving is: 1/2 cup chopped raw, nonleafy vegetables; 1 cup of leafy, raw vegetables; 1/2 cup cooked vegetables; 1/2 cup cooked legumes; 1 small baked potato; and 3/4 cup vegetable juice.[4]

SCALLOPED NEW POTATOES

INGREDIENTS

1	medium onion, chopped
3	tablespoons margarine
2	garlic cloves, minced
2	tablespoons flour
2	cups skim milk
4	cups sliced new potatoes
3/4	cup grated Parmesan cheese
2	teaspoons Dijon mustard
1	teaspoon reduced-sodium Worcestershire sauce
■	Freshly ground white pepper to taste

METHOD

■ Combine the onion, margarine and garlic in a microwave-safe bowl. Microwave on High for 1 to 2 minutes or until the onion is tender. Stir in the flour. Microwave on High for 30 seconds. Whisk in the skim milk.

■ Microwave on High for 2 to 4 minutes or until slightly thickened, stirring twice. Stir in the new potatoes, cheese, Dijon mustard, Worcestershire sauce and pepper.

■ Microwave, covered, on High for 6 to 8 minutes or until the potatoes are tender, stirring twice.

Yield: 6 servings

Approx Per Serving: Cal 245; Prot 11 g; Carbo 29 g; T Fat 10 g; 36% Calories from Fat; Chol 11 mg; Fiber 2 g; Sod 391 mg

Potato Puree with Cheese

From the recipe files of Dr. Sara M. Jordan.
Modified by Lahey Clinic Executive Chef John R. Di Sessa, C.E.C.

Ingredients

5	medium potatoes, peeled, cut into quarters
1	cup skim milk, scalded
1	tablespoon margarine, softened
1/2	teaspoon salt
1/4	cup shredded reduced-fat Jarlsberg cheese

Method

- Combine the potatoes with enough water to cover in a saucepan. Bring to a boil. Boil until tender; drain.
- Mash the potatoes in a mixing bowl with a fork. Beat at low speed until blended. Add the skim milk, margarine and salt gradually, beating constantly until light and fluffy.
- Layer the potato mixture and cheese 1/3 at a time in a buttered baking dish, ending with the cheese. Bake at 400 degrees until brown and bubbly and the internal temperature registers 165 degrees.

Yield: 4 servings

Approx Per Serving: Cal 185; Prot 8 g; Carbo 30 g; T Fat 4 g; 19% Calories from Fat; Chol 4 mg; Fiber 2 g; Sod 397 mg

CANTONESE SHRIMP-FRIED RICE

■

INGREDIENTS

3	eggs
2	green onions, finely chopped
3	tablespoons vegetable oil
4	ounces deveined peeled small fresh shrimp
1/2	cup finely chopped cooked ham or pork
1/2	cup finely chopped bamboo shoots
1/2	cup frozen green peas, thawed
2	ounces small fresh mushrooms
2	to 3 cups cold cooked white rice
1 1/2	tablespoons reduced-sodium soy sauce

METHOD

■ Whisk the eggs in a bowl just until blended. Stir in half the green onions. Heat a nonstick skillet over medium heat. Add 1 tablespoon of the oil. Heat until hot. Add the egg mixture and scramble. Remove the scrambled eggs to a platter.

■ Heat the remaining 2 tablespoons oil in the skillet over high heat. Add the remaining green onions, shrimp, ham, bamboo shoots, peas and mushrooms. Stir-fry for 1 to 2 minutes. Add the rice and soy sauce, stirring until each grain of rice is separated and the mixture is heated through. Add the scrambled eggs and stir to break the eggs into bite-size pieces. Serve immediately.

Yield: 4 servings

Approx Per Serving: Cal 378; Prot 19 g; Carbo 39 g; T Fat 16 g; 38% Calories from Fat; Chol 209 mg; Fiber 2 g; Sod 555 mg

Squash and Apple Medley

■

INGREDIENTS

2   medium acorn squash
2   unpeeled cooking apples,
    cut into wedges
2/3 cup apple juice

2   tablespoons margarine
1/4 cup packed brown sugar
1/4 teaspoon apple pie spice
1/8 teaspoon salt

METHOD

■ Cut the squash crosswise into 1-inch rings and discard the seeds. Cut the rings into halves. Arrange in a single layer in a 9×13-inch baking pan.

■ Bake, covered, at 350 degrees for 40 minutes or until tender-crisp. Arrange the apple wedges over the squash.

■ Combine the apple juice, margarine, brown sugar, apple pie spice and salt in a saucepan. Bring to a boil; reduce heat. Simmer for 3 minutes, stirring frequently. Spoon over the prepared layers.

■ Bake for 10 minutes longer or until the apples are tender, basting with the pan juices frequently.

Yield: 6 servings

Approx Per Serving: Cal 166; Prot 1 g; Carbo 34 g; T Fat 4 g; 21% Calories from Fat; Chol 0 mg; Fiber 3 g; Sod 102 mg

CURRIED SWEET POTATOES

■

INGREDIENTS

3   pounds sweet potatoes, peeled

6   tablespoons margarine, melted

1/2   cup packed light brown sugar

2   teaspoons curry powder

METHOD

■ Cut the sweet potatoes into 1/2-inch slices. Arrange in a single layer in a baking pan.

■ Mix the margarine, brown sugar and curry powder in a bowl. Spoon over the sweet potatoes. Bake at 350 degrees for 25 to 30 minutes or until tender.

Yield: 8 servings

Approx Per Serving: Cal 234; Prot 2 g; Carbo 39 g; T Fat 9 g; 32% Calories from Fat; Chol 0 mg; Fiber 3 g; Sod 115 mg

MICROWAVE ZUCCHINI BOATS

■

INGREDIENTS

3   medium zucchini

1   tablespoon margarine

1   tablespoon parsley flakes

1   tablespoon olive oil

1   tablespoon minced onion

1   garlic clove, minced

1   large tomato, chopped

1/2   cup fine bread crumbs

■   Salt and freshly ground pepper to taste

1/3   cup grated Parmesan cheese

METHOD

■ Cut the zucchini into halves lengthwise. Scoop out the pulp, leaving a 1/4-inch shell. Chop the pulp. Arrange the shells cut side up in a microwave-safe dish.

■ Combine the next 5 ingredients in a microwave-safe bowl. Microwave on High until the margarine melts. Stir in the reserved pulp, tomato, bread crumbs, salt and pepper. Spoon into the shells. Microwave, covered with waxed paper, on High for 5 minutes. Sprinkle with the cheese. Microwave on High for 1 minute longer.

Yield: 6 servings

Approx Per Serving: Cal 121; Prot 5 g; Carbo 12 g; T Fat 7 g; 47% Calories from Fat; Chol 4 mg; Fiber 2 g; Sod 210 mg

SESAME VEGETABLE STIR-FRY

■

INGREDIENTS

1	tablespoon sesame seeds
1	tablespoon olive oil
1	medium onion, cut into wedges
1	garlic clove, minced
1	cup fresh or thawed frozen broccoli florets
1	cup fresh or thawed frozen cauliflorets
1	small yellow squash or zucchini, sliced
1	tablespoon soy or teriyaki sauce
1	tablespoon lemon pepper
1 1/2	teaspoons sesame oil
2	small tomatoes, cut into wedges

METHOD

■ Spread the sesame seeds in a single layer on an ungreased baking sheet. Toast at 350 degrees for 10 to 15 minutes or until light brown, stirring once or twice.

■ Heat a wok over medium-high heat. Add the olive oil. Stir-fry the onion and garlic in the olive oil for 2 minutes; push to the side. Add the broccoli and cauliflower.

■ Stir-fry for 2 minutes; push to the side. Add the squash. Stir-fry for 2 to 3 minutes or until of the desired degree of crispness.

■ Stir the onion, garlic, broccoli, cauliflower and squash together. Add a mixture of the soy sauce, lemon pepper and sesame oil and mix well. Stir in the tomatoes.

■ Cook, covered, over low heat for 1 minute. Transfer the vegetables to a serving bowl. Sprinkle with the sesame seeds.

Yield: 6 servings

Approx Per Serving: Cal 67; Prot 2 g; Carbo 6 g; T Fat 5 g; 56% Calories from Fat; Chol 0 mg; Fiber 2 g; Sod 463 mg

■

You can also obtain calcium from plant-based foods such as broccoli, bok choy, collard greens, kale, mustard greens, tofu prepared with calcium, and products like specially-fortified orange juice, cereal, and soy milk. All have the added benefit of cancer fighting nutrients.[2]

BUFFALO MOZZARELLA AND VEGETABLE TERRINE

■

INGREDIENTS

1/2	ounce unflavored gelatin	1	tablespoon dry marsala
1	to 2 tablespoons cold water	6	Belgian endive leaves
6	(1/8-inch) eggplant slices, grilled	6	radicchio leaves
6	ounces buffalo mozzarella cheese, thinly sliced	6	arugula leaves
6	sun-dried tomatoes, blanched	6	baby red oak leaves
6	oyster mushroom caps	6	tablespoons extra-virgin olive oil
6	shiitake mushroom caps	2	tablespoons balsamic vinegar
1	ounce pesto	1/3	ounce shallots, minced
1/2	cup chicken consommé, heated	1/8	ounce minced garlic
		■	Salt and pepper to taste

METHOD

■ Line a mold with plastic wrap. Mix the gelatin and water in a small bowl. Let stand until softened. Line the prepared mold with some of the eggplant slices. Layer with some of the cheese. Layer the remaining eggplant, sun-dried tomatoes, mushrooms and remaining cheese over the prepared layers, brushing each layer with some of the pesto.

■ Combine the gelatin mixture, consommé and wine in a bowl and mix well. Spoon over the prepared layers. Chill, covered, for 4 hours.

■ Toss the endive, radicchio, arugula and red oak leaves in a bowl. Drizzle with a mixture of the olive oil, balsamic vinegar, shallots, garlic, salt and pepper.

■ Arrange the greens evenly on 6 salad plates. Cut the terrine into 1/8-inch slices with an electric knife. Arrange the slices over the greens. May also serve with a roasted red pepper vinaigrette.

Yield: 6 servings

Approx Per Serving: Cal 295; Prot 11 g; Carbo 13 g; T Fat 22 g; 67% Calories from Fat; Chol 24 mg; Fiber 3 g; Sod 454 mg

Banana Biscuits

Ingredients

1	cup whole wheat flour
1	cup all-purpose flour
2	teaspoons baking powder
1	tablespoon sugar
1/4	teaspoon baking soda
1/4	teaspoon cinnamon
1/8	teaspoon nutmeg
1/8	teaspoon allspice
1/4	cup (1/2 stick) margarine
1/2	cup mashed banana
1/4	cup vanilla reduced-fat yogurt
2	tablespoons skim milk
1	to 2 tablespoons all-purpose flour

Method

■ Combine the whole wheat flour, 1 cup all-purpose flour, baking powder, sugar, baking soda, cinnamon, nutmeg and allspice in a bowl and mix well. Cut in the margarine until crumbly. Stir in the banana and yogurt. Add the skim milk, stirring just until moistened.

■ Let rest for 5 minutes. Turn the dough onto a floured surface. Knead 4 times, adding 1 to 2 tablespoons all-purpose flour as needed to make an easily handled dough. Roll 1/2 inch thick. Cut with a 2-inch round cutter.

■ Arrange the biscuits on a baking sheet coated with nonstick cooking spray. Bake at 450 degrees for 8 minutes or until golden brown.

Yield: 16 biscuits

Approx Per Biscuit: Cal 97; Prot 2 g; Carbo 15 g; T Fat 3 g; 29% Calories from Fat; Chol <1 mg; Fiber 1 g; Sod 118 mg

The terms enriched and fortified often need clarifying. Enriched means adding back nutrients that were lost during food processing. For example, B vitamins, lost when wheat is refined, are added back to white flour. Fortified means adding nutrients that weren't present originally. For example, milk is fortified with vitamin D, a nutrient that helps your body absorb the calcium and phosphorus in milk. And according to a new law, most enriched grain products are now being fortified with folic acid to reduce the incidence of certain birth defects.[4]

CRANBERRY BREAD

INGREDIENTS

2 cups sifted flour	2 tablespoons canola oil
3/4 cup sugar	1 egg, beaten, or 1/4 cup egg
1 1/2 teaspoons baking powder	substitute
1/2 teaspoon baking soda	2 cups fresh cranberries,
1 teaspoon salt	coarsely chopped
■ Juice and grated zest of 1 orange	1/2 cup chopped walnuts

METHOD

■ Sift the flour, sugar, baking powder, baking soda and salt into a bowl and mix well. Combine the orange juice, orange zest and canola oil in a 2-cup measure with enough water to measure 3/4 cup. Add the egg and mix well. Add to the dry ingredients, stirring just until moistened. Fold in the cranberries and walnuts.

■ Spoon the batter into a greased 5×9-inch loaf pan, spreading the batter evenly and making the corners and sides slightly higher than the center. Bake at 350 degrees for 50 to 60 minutes or until the loaf tests done. Remove to a wire rack to cool.

■ Store, wrapped in foil, at room temperature for 8 to 10 hours before slicing. The recipe will make 16 muffins if desired.

Yield: 12 servings

Approx Per Serving: Cal 189; Prot 3 g; Carbo 31 g; T Fat 6 g; 28% Calories from Fat; Chol 18 mg; Fiber 2 g; Sod 314 mg

APPLE WALNUT MUFFINS

■

INGREDIENTS

1¹/₂ cups flour

1   cup raisin bran cereal

²/₃   cup sugar

¹/₃   cup graham cracker crumbs

1¹/₄ teaspoons baking soda

¹/₄   teaspoon salt

1   cup buttermilk

2   tablespoons margarine, melted

1   egg, lightly beaten

1   cup finely chopped peeled baking apple

¹/₃   cup chopped walnuts, toasted

2   tablespoons sugar

1   teaspoon cinnamon

1   tablespoon margarine, melted

METHOD

■ Combine the flour, cereal, ²/₃ cup sugar, graham cracker crumbs, baking soda and salt in a bowl and mix well. Make a well in the center of the mixture. Add a mixture of the buttermilk, 2 tablespoons margarine and egg to the well and stir just until moistened. Combine the apple, walnuts, 2 tablespoons sugar, cinnamon and 1 tablespoon margarine in a bowl and mix well.

■ Spray 12 muffin cups with nonstick cooking spray. Spoon 2 tablespoons of the batter into each muffin cup. Divide the apple mixture evenly among the muffin cups. Top with the remaining batter.

■ Bake at 350 degrees for 25 minutes or until the muffins test done. Remove to a wire rack immediately.

Yield: 1 dozen muffins

Approx Per Muffin: Cal 205; Prot 4 g; Carbo 35 g; T Fat 6 g; 26% Calories from Fat; Chol 18 mg; Fiber 2 g; Sod 290 mg

---

■

Unsweetened applesauce, puréed pears, apple butter, and puréed dark colored fruits may be used as substitutions for oils in most baked goods. Replace the oil with the same amount of fruit.[5]

MORNING GLORY MUFFINS

■

INGREDIENTS

2	cups flour	1 1/2	cups grated carrots
3/4	cup sugar	1	(8-ounce) can juice-pack crushed pineapple, drained
2	teaspoons baking soda		
2	teaspoons cinnamon	1	cup grated or finely chopped apple
3/4	cup plus 2 tablespoons pineapple juice or orange juice	1/2	cup chopped pecans
		1/2	cup raisins
2	tablespoons canola oil	1/2	cup shredded coconut
3	eggs, lightly beaten, or 3/4 cup egg substitute		

METHOD

■ Combine the flour, sugar, baking soda and cinnamon in a bowl and mix well. Combine the pineapple juice, canola oil and eggs in a bowl and mix well. Add to the flour mixture, stirring just until moistened. Fold in the carrots, pineapple, apple, pecans, raisins and coconut.

■ Spoon the batter into 18 paper-lined muffin cups. Bake at 400 degrees for 20 minutes. You may substitute a mixture of 1 1/3 cups flour and 2/3 cup oat bran for 2 cups flour.

Yield: 18 muffins

Approx Per Muffin: Cal 178; Prot 3 g; Carbo 30 g; T Fat 6 g; 28% Calories from Fat; Chol 35 mg; Fiber 2 g; Sod 162 mg

DILLY BREAD

■

INGREDIENTS

1   envelope dry yeast
3/4 cup warm (105- to 115-degree) water
2¹/2 cups flour
1¹/2 tablespoons instant minced onion
1   tablespoon sugar
1   teaspoon dillseeds
¹/2 teaspoon salt
1   cup 1% cottage cheese

METHOD

■ Combine the yeast and warm water in a bowl and mix well.
Let stand for 5 minutes.

■ Combine the flour, onion, sugar, dillseeds and salt in a food
processor container fitted with a steel blade. Process for
5 seconds. Add the cottage cheese. Process for 10 seconds.
Scrape the side of the bowl.

■ Add the yeast mixture through the food chute, processing
constantly for 10 seconds. Spoon the batter into a bowl
coated with nonstick cooking spray. Let rise, covered, in a
warm place for 1 hour or until doubled in bulk; stir.

■ Spoon into a 9×9-inch baking dish sprayed with nonstick
cooking spray. Let rise, covered, in a warm place for
45 minutes or until doubled in bulk.

■ Bake at 350 degrees for 40 minutes or until brown. Cool
in baking dish for 5 minutes. Remove to a wire rack to cool
completely.

Yield: 12 servings

*Approx Per Serving: Cal 116; Prot 5 g; Carbo 22 g; T Fat <1 g;
4% Calories from Fat; Chol 1 mg; Fiber 1 g; Sod 174 mg*

■

*Sugar adds more than taste
to yeast breads. Sugars are
the food for yeast, allowing
the dough to rise. However,
the yeast doesn't consume
all of the sugar. The rest
adds flavor and contributes
to the aroma and delicate-
brown color of the crust.[4]*

OAT AND WALNUT BUTTERMILK BRAID

From Lahey Clinic Executive Chef John R. Di Sessa, C.E.C.

■

INGREDIENTS

½	cup lukewarm water	2	tablespoons vegetable oil
¼	cup honey	2	teaspoons salt
1	envelope dry yeast	1	cup chopped walnuts
2	cups buttermilk	1	egg
4⅓	cups bread flour	2	tablespoons milk
2	cups old-fashioned oats	3	to 4 tablespoons old-fashioned oats
1	cup whole wheat flour		

METHOD

■ Combine the lukewarm water and honey in a bowl and mix well. Sprinkle the yeast over the top. Let stand for 8 minutes or until foamy.

■ Heat the buttermilk in a saucepan to 100 degrees or until lukewarm. Stir in the yeast mixture. Add 2 cups of the bread flour, 2 cups oats, whole wheat flour, oil and salt and mix until smooth. Add enough of the remaining bread flour to make an easily handled dough. Let rise, covered, for 15 minutes.

■ Knead the dough on a lightly floured surface for 10 minutes or until smooth and elastic, adding the remaining bread flour as needed. Knead in the walnuts. Place the dough in a greased bowl, turning to coat the surface. Let rise, covered with a tea towel, in a warm place for 50 minutes or until doubled in bulk. Punch the dough down.

■ Turn the dough onto an oiled surface. Knead briefly. Divide the dough into 3 portions. Roll each portion into a 16-inch rope. Shape into a braid on an oiled baking sheet. Tuck the ends under and pinch to seal. Let rise, covered with a tea towel, in a warm place for 45 minutes or until almost doubled in bulk.

■ Whisk the egg and milk in a bowl. Brush the braid with the egg mixture. Sprinkle with 3 to 4 tablespoons oats.

■ Bake at 375 degrees for 50 minutes or until a wooden pick inserted in the center comes out clean and the bread is golden brown. May be prepared 1 day in advance and stored, tightly wrapped, at room temperature.

Yield: 16 servings

Approx Per Serving: Cal 312; Prot 10 g; Carbo 49 g; T Fat 9 g; 25% Calories from Fat; Chol 15 mg; Fiber 4 g; Sod 330 mg

BASIC PASTA DOUGH

From Lahey Clinic Executive Chef John R. Di Sessa, C.E.C.

■

INGREDIENTS

3   pounds 10 ounces semolina flour   11   to 12 ounces water
10 ounces egg whites (about 10 egg
    whites)

METHOD

■ Combine the flour, egg whites and water in a mixing bowl fitted with a dough
  hook. Beat until the mixture is mealy, adding additional water or flour if needed
  for the desired consistency. Shape the dough into a ball and wrap tightly in
  plastic wrap.

■ Let rest for 1 hour. Working in small manageable portions, roll the dough through
  the widest part of a pasta machine and then fold into thirds. Repeat the process
  3 or 4 times to knead. Pass the dough through successively smaller settings until the
  desired thickness is reached. Cut into desired shapes.

■ Bring 1 gallon of water to a rolling boil in a stockpot for each pound of pasta. Add
  the pasta, stirring gently to separate the strands. Cook just until al dente; drain.

VARIATIONS

■ For Spinach Pasta, add 1¼ pounds puréed raw spinach and decrease the water by
  5 ounces. For Pumpkin, Beet or Carrot Pasta, cook 1¼ pounds pumpkin, beets or
  carrots until most of the moisture has evaporated. Drain and purée. Add the purée
  and just enough of the water for the desired consistency. For Tomato Pasta, heat
  8 ounces tomato paste in a sauté pan until most of the moisture has evaporated.
  Reduce the addition of the water by about 3 ounces and add the water gradually
  until the desired consistency is achieved. For Fresh Herb Pasta, add 3 tablespoons
  chopped fresh herbs to the dough. For Spice Pasta, add 3 tablespoons crushed
  spices to the dough.

Yield: 10 (8-ounce) pasta servings

*Approx Per Serving: Cal 606; Prot 24 g; Carbo 120 g; T Fat 2 g; 3% Calories from Fat;
Chol 0 mg; Fiber 6 g; Sod 48 mg
Nutritional information does not include variations.*

ENTREES

BEEF STEW

INGREDIENTS

1 pound beef stew meat, trimmed
8 new red potatoes
2 medium carrots, sliced
1/2 onion, sliced, separated
   into rings
3 garlic cloves, minced
1 cup dry sherry

2 tablespoons finely grated orange
   zest
1/2 cup orange juice
2 teaspoons reduced-sodium soy sauce
1/2 teaspoon freshly ground pepper
1/4 cup cold water
2 tablespoons cornstarch

METHOD

■ Combine the stew meat, potatoes, carrots, onion and garlic in a stockpot. Whisk the sherry, orange zest, orange juice, soy sauce and pepper in a bowl. Add to the stockpot and mix gently, adding water if needed to cover the vegetables.

■ Simmer, covered, for 1 1/2 hours or until the vegetables are tender and the beef is of the desired degree of doneness, stirring occasionally. Drain the liquid into a bowl and skim. Bring 2 cups of the liquid to a boil in a saucepan, discarding the remaining liquid. Stir in a mixture of the cold water and cornstarch. Cook until thickened, stirring constantly. Pour over the beef mixture and mix gently. Serve immediately.

Yield: 4 servings

Approx Per Serving: Cal 462; Prot 27 g; Carbo 61 g; T Fat 8 g; 16% Calories from Fat; Chol 70 mg; Fiber 6 g; Sod 324 mg

TRINIDAD BEEF STEW

■

INGREDIENTS

3   pounds beef bottom round, trimmed
3   tablespoons flour
1   tablespoon vegetable oil
2   (16-ounce) cans no-salt-added chopped tomatoes
3   cups sliced onions
1¼ teaspoons pepper
1   teaspoon salt
2   cups water
⅓   cup white vinegar
3   tablespoons molasses
2½ cups thinly sliced carrots
½   cup raisins
½   teaspoon ginger

METHOD

■ Coat the beef with the flour. Brown the beef in the oil in
a large saucepan. Add the undrained tomatoes, onions,
pepper and salt and mix well. Stir in a mixture of the water,
vinegar and molasses.

■ Simmer, covered, for 1¼ hours or until the beef is tender,
stirring occasionally. Stir in the carrots, raisins and ginger.
Simmer, for 30 minutes longer or until the carrots are
tender, stirring occasionally.

■ Remove the beef to a platter and shred. Return the
shredded beef to the saucepan and mix gently. Cook just
until heated through, stirring frequently.

Yield: 9 servings

*Approx Per Serving: Cal 462; Prot 36 g; Carbo 31 g; T Fat 22 g;
42% Calories from Fat; Chol 112 mg; Fiber 3 g; Sod 350 mg*

■

*Tenderize leaner
cuts of meat with
marinades of lemon juice,
flavored vinegar, wine,
or fruit juices.[5]*

SZECHUAN SHREDDED BEEF

INGREDIENTS

2	tablespoons sesame oil
12	ounces beef flank steak, shredded
1	tablespoon sake
1	tablespoon chile bean paste
1	tablespoon hoisin sauce
1	tablespoon sugar
1	tablespoon sake
1	garlic clove, minced
1/2	teaspoon salt
1	large carrot, shredded
2	to 3 ribs celery, shredded
2	green onions with tops, finely chopped
2	teaspoons minced gingerroot
1/2	teaspoon freshly ground Szechuan pepper
1	teaspoon chili oil

METHOD

■ Heat a wok over high heat. Add the sesame oil. Heat until hot. Add the beef and 1 tablespoon sake. Stir-fry until the beef strands separate. Reduce the heat. Drain any excess liquid. Stir-fry until all of the moisture has evaporated.

■ Stir in the bean paste, hoisin sauce, sugar, 1 tablespoon sake, garlic and salt. Stir-fry for several seconds. Increase the heat to high.

■ Add the carrot and celery. Stir-fry for 1 minute. Add the green onions, gingerroot, pepper and chili oil. Stir-fry for 1 minute. Serve immediately.

Yield: 4 servings

Approx Per Serving: Cal 266; Prot 19 g; Carbo 12 g; T Fat 15 g; 50% Calories from Fat; Chol 44 mg; Fiber 2 g; Sod 450 mg

Ginger-Braised Beef

■

INGREDIENTS

1¹/₂ pounds beef stew meat

4 thin slices gingerroot

3 tablespoons sake

1 tablespoon brandy

2 tablespoons vegetable oil

¹/₄ cup reduced-sodium soy sauce

1 tablespoon sugar

1 teaspoon five-spice powder

METHOD

■ Combine the beef, gingerroot, sake and brandy with enough water to cover in a saucepan and mix well. Bring to a boil over medium heat; skim off the foam. Reduce the heat.

■ Simmer, covered, for 45 minutes, stirring occasionally. Remove the beef with a slotted spoon to a platter, reserving half the pan juices. Pat the beef dry with paper towels.

■ Heat the oil in a skillet over high heat. Add the beef. Stir-fry until brown on all sides. Stir in the reserved pan juices, soy sauce, sugar and five-spice powder; reduce the heat.

■ Simmer, covered, for 40 to 45 minutes or until the beef is tender, stirring occasionally. Remove the beef with a slotted spoon to a cutting board, reserving the pan juices. Cut the beef into thin slices. Return the beef to the skillet and mix well. Cook just until heated through. Spoon into a serving bowl. Serve hot or cold.

Yield: 4 servings

Approx Per Serving: Cal 357; Prot 34 g; Carbo 7 g; T Fat 19 g; 48% Calories from Fat; Chol 105 mg; Fiber <1 g; Sod 815 mg

Fiesta Meatball Stew

INGREDIENTS

1   pound ground chuck

1   (4-ounce) can chopped green
    chiles, drained

1/4 cup soft bread crumbs

1   egg, lightly beaten

1/2 teaspoon cumin

1/4 teaspoon pepper

2 1/4 cups water

1/3 cup flour

1   (15-ounce) can no-salt-added
    diced tomatoes

1   (15-ounce) can black beans,
    drained, rinsed

1   (10-ounce) package frozen whole
    kernel corn

1   tablespoon chili powder

1   teaspoon beef bouillon granules

1   teaspoon oregano

METHOD

- Combine the ground chuck, 3 tablespoons of the chiles, bread crumbs, egg, cumin and pepper in a bowl and mix well. Shape into meatballs, using 2 teaspoons of the ground chuck mixture per meatball.
- Arrange the meatballs in a single layer on a broiler rack sprayed with nonstick cooking spray. Place the rack in a broiler pan. Broil 5 to 6 inches from the heat source for 5 minutes; turn. Broil for 4 minutes longer or until brown. Drain and pat the meatballs dry with paper towels.
- Combine the water and flour in a large saucepan and mix well. Cook over medium heat until thickened, stirring constantly. Add the meatballs, remaining chiles, undrained tomatoes, beans, corn, chili powder, bouillon granules and oregano and mix gently.
- Bring to a boil; reduce heat. Simmer, covered, for 30 minutes, stirring occasionally.

Yield: 7 (1-cup) servings

Approx Per Serving: Cal 280; Prot 21 g; Carbo 26 g; T Fat 11 g; 34% Calories from Fat; Chol 77 mg; Fiber 6 g; Sod 578 mg

Tamale Pie

■

INGREDIENTS

8   ounces extra-lean ground beef
3/4 cup chopped onion
1   garlic clove, minced
1/2 cup chopped green bell pepper
2   (8-ounce) cans no-salt-added tomato sauce
1   (16-ounce) can no-salt-added pinto beans,
     drained, rinsed
1   (16-ounce) can no-salt-added whole kernel corn,
     drained, rinsed
1/4 cup sliced drained black olives
2   to 3 tablespoons salsa
2   teaspoons chili powder
2 1/2 cups water
1   cup yellow cornmeal
1/4 teaspoon (or less) salt
1/2 cup shredded part-skim mozzarella cheese

METHOD

■ Brown the ground beef with the onion and garlic in a
nonstick skillet, stirring until the ground beef is crumbly;
drain. Stir in the green pepper, tomato sauce, beans, corn,
black olives, salsa and chili powder. Spoon into a 10×10-
inch baking pan.

■ Combine the water, cornmeal and salt in a saucepan and
mix well. Bring to a boil, stirring constantly. Boil until
thickened, stirring constantly.

■ Spread the cornmeal mixture over the prepared layer. Bake
at 375 degrees for 45 minutes. Sprinkle with the cheese.
Bake for 15 minutes longer.

Yield: 6 servings

*Approx Per Serving: Cal 306; Prot 19 g; Carbo 47 g; T Fat 6 g;
17% Calories from Fat; Chol 21 mg; Fiber 9 g; Sod 292 mg*

■

*Some evidence indicates
that diets high in fat may
increase the risk of cancers
of the colon, breast,
prostate, and the lining of
the uterus. Diets low in fat
may reduce these risks while
they help to control weight
and also reduce risk of
heart attack and stroke.[6]*

BEEF STOCK

■

INGREDIENTS

4	pounds uncooked meaty beef bones	6	sprigs of parsley
3	quarts water	10	peppercorns
2	large onions, chopped	4	whole cloves
2	large carrots, coarsely chopped	1	bay leaf
2	large ribs celery with leaves, chopped	■	Salt to taste
2	garlic cloves	2	cups water
		2	tablespoons red wine vinegar

METHOD

■ Roast the bones in a roasting pan at 450 degrees for 30 minutes, turning once. Combine the 3 quarts water, onions, carrots, celery, garlic, parsley, peppercorns, cloves, bay leaf and salt in a stockpot. Bring to a boil; reduce heat. Add the roasted bones and mix well.

■ Discard the fat from the roasting pan. Stir in 2 cups water with a wooden spoon, scraping the bottom and side of the pan to dislodge any brown sediment. Stir into the stockpot mixture. Bring to a boil; reduce heat.

■ Simmer, partially covered, for 3 hours, stirring occasionally and skimming the foam as needed. Stir in the wine vinegar. Simmer, partially covered, for 2 hours longer, stirring occasionally. Strain, discarding the solids. The broth may be cooked longer at this point to intensify the flavor. Chill and spoon off the hardened fat.

Yield: 14 (1-cup) servings

Approx Per Serving: Cal 20; Prot 5 g; Carbo 0 g; T Fat 0 g; 0% Calories from Fat; Chol 0 mg; Fiber 0 g; Sod 70 mg

PORK MEDALLIONS

■

INGREDIENTS

2   teaspoons olive oil
1   (1-pound) pork tenderloin, trimmed
1/4 cup thinly sliced green onions
2/3 cup dry white wine
1   cup beef consommé
3   tablespoons Dijon mustard
3   tablespoons margarine
1/8 teaspoon sugar
1   red bell pepper, julienned
1   yellow bell pepper, julienned
1   teaspoon balsamic vinegar

METHOD

■ Heat the olive oil in a skillet until hot. Add the pork and green onions. Sauté for 5 to 8 minutes or until the pork is brown on all sides, turning frequently. Add the white wine. Simmer for 10 to 15 minutes or until the pork is cooked through. Remove the pork to a platter, reserving the pan drippings. Cover to keep warm.

■ Stir the consommé into the reserved pan drippings. Bring to a boil. Boil until the liquid is reduced to 1/2 cup. Whisk in the Dijon mustard, 2 tablespoons of the margarine and sugar. Cut the pork into 1/2-inch slices. Pour the mustard sauce over the pork. Cover to keep warm.

■ Melt the remaining 1 tablespoon margarine in the skillet. Add the red pepper and yellow pepper. Stir-fry the bell peppers over medium-high heat for 3 minutes or until tender-crisp. Stir in the vinegar. Arrange the bell peppers around the pork.

Yield: 4 servings

Approx Per Serving: Cal 310; Prot 28 g; Carbo 7 g; T Fat 16 g; 46% Calories from Fat; Chol 67 mg; Fiber 1 g; Sod 756 mg

■

To reduce fat in your diet, choose more often the lean cuts of beef, lamb, and pork and less often the high-fat cuts. Trim away all the visible fat before you cook the meat and again before you consume the meat. If you eat luncheon and variety meats, choose those that are labeled reduced-fat. Choose more often poultry, such as chicken and turkey, and remove the skin and visible fat before cooking.[6]

HONEY SESAME TENDERLOIN

■

INGREDIENTS

$1/2$ cup soy sauce
1 tablespoon grated gingerroot, or 1 teaspoon
   dried ginger
1 tablespoon toasted sesame oil
2 garlic cloves, minced
1 (1-pound) pork tenderloin
$1/4$ cup honey
2 tablespoons brown sugar
$1/4$ cup sesame seeds

METHOD

■ Combine the soy sauce, gingerroot, sesame oil and garlic
in a sealable plastic bag. Add the pork and seal tightly. Toss
to coat. Marinate in the refrigerator for 2 to 10 hours,
turning occasionally. Drain the pork and pat dry; discard
the marinade.

■ Combine the honey and brown sugar in a shallow dish and
mix well. Roll the pork in the honey mixture and coat with
the sesame seeds.

■ Place the pork in a shallow baking pan lined with foil.
Bake at 400 degrees for 20 to 30 minutes or until a meat
thermometer registers 160 degrees. Remove the pork to a
platter. Cut into thin slices.

Yield: 4 servings

*Approx Per Serving: Cal 340; Prot 29 g; Carbo 28 g; T Fat 13 g;
33% Calories from Fat; Chol 67 mg; Fiber 1 g; Sod 2686 mg
Nutritional information includes the entire amount of marinade,
but the sodium content would be lower as not all would be
absorbed into the meat.*

MARINATED PORK TENDERLOIN

■

INGREDIENTS

2	tablespoons lime juice	1	teaspoon crushed red pepper
2	tablespoons reduced-sodium soy sauce	2	garlic cloves, crushed
2	tablespoons hoisin sauce	1	(1-pound) pork tenderloin, trimmed
1	tablespoon minced gingerroot		

METHOD

■ Combine the lime juice, soy sauce, hoisin sauce, gingerroot, red pepper and garlic in a sealable plastic bag. Add the pork and seal tightly. Toss to coat. Marinate in the refrigerator for 2 hours, turning occasionally.

■ Drain the pork, reserving the marinade. Arrange the pork on a grill rack sprayed with nonstick cooking spray. Grill, covered, over medium-hot coals for 30 minutes or until a meat thermometer registers 160 degrees, turning and basting with the reserved marinade occasionally. Remove the pork to a platter. Cut into 1/4-inch slices.

Yield: 4 servings

Approx Per Serving: Cal 169; Prot 25 g; Carbo 6 g; T Fat 4 g; 24% Calories from Fat; Chol 67 mg; Fiber <1 g; Sod 430 mg
Nutritional information includes the entire amount of marinade.

GINGER ORANGE PORK

INGREDIENTS

1/2   cup plain reduced-fat yogurt
1   tablespoon minced gingerroot
1   tablespoon orange juice
2   teaspoons coriander
1/2   teaspoon cumin
1/4   teaspoon crushed red pepper
1/4   teaspoon salt
1   (1-pound) pork tenderloin, trimmed

METHOD

■ Combine the yogurt, gingerroot, orange juice, coriander, cumin, red pepper and salt in a shallow dish and mix well. Add the pork, turning to coat. Marinate, covered, in the refrigerator for 8 hours, turning occasionally.

■ Drain the pork, reserving the marinade. Arrange the pork on a rack sprayed with nonstick cooking spray. Place the rack in a shallow baking pan. Bake at 400 degrees for 30 minutes or until a meat thermometer registers 160 degrees, basting every 15 minutes with the reserved marinade. Remove the pork to a serving platter. Slice as desired.

Yield: 4 servings

Approx Per Serving: Cal 161; Prot 26 g; Carbo 3 g; T Fat 5 g; 27% Calories from Fat; Chol 69 mg; Fiber <1 g; Sod 215 mg Nutritional information includes the entire amount of marinade.

Teriyaki Pork Tenderloin

■

INGREDIENTS

1 (1-pound) pork tenderloin, trimmed
2 tablespoons wine or beer
2 tablespoons reduced-sodium soy sauce
2 teaspoons minced gingerroot
2 garlic cloves, minced

METHOD

■ Arrange the tenderloin in a shallow baking dish. Combine the wine, soy sauce, gingerroot and garlic in a bowl and mix well. Pour over the pork, turning to coat. Marinate, covered, in the refrigerator for 2 hours, turning occasionally.

■ Drain the pork, reserving the marinade. Arrange the pork on a rack sprayed with nonstick cooking spray. Place the rack in a shallow baking pan. Bake at 400 degrees for 30 minutes or until a meat thermometer registers 160 degrees, basting occasionally with the reserved marinade.

Yield: 4 servings

Approx Per Serving: Cal 154; Prot 25 g; Carbo 2 g; T Fat 4 g; 25% Calories from Fat; Chol 67 mg; Fiber <1 g; Sod 301 mg Nutritional information includes the entire amount of marinade.

■

Saturated fatty acids are fatty acids that have all the hydrogen they can hold on their chemical chains. They come mainly from animal sources, such as meat, poultry, butter, and whole milk, and from coconut, palm, and palm kernel oils. Foods high in saturated fatty acids are firm at room temperature.[4]

BOILED PORK WITH SPICY GINGER SAUCE

INGREDIENTS

1	(1³/₄-pound) boneless pork roast
¹/₄	cup reduced-sodium soy sauce
1	tablespoon toasted sesame oil
1	teaspoon minced gingerroot
1	teaspoon finely chopped green onions
¹/₂	teaspoon minced garlic
1	teaspoon chili sauce

METHOD

■ Combine the pork with enough water to cover in a saucepan. Bring to a boil; reduce heat. Simmer, covered, for 1 hour or until the pork is cooked through; drain. Transfer to a serving platter. Cool slightly.

■ Combine the soy sauce, sesame oil, gingerroot, green onions, garlic and chili sauce in a bowl and mix well. Slice the pork across the grain into the desired thickness. Drizzle with the sauce or serve the sauce separately.

Yield: 6 servings

Approx Per Serving: Cal 225; Prot 31 g; Carbo 2 g; T Fat 9 g; 39% Calories from Fat; Chol 77 mg; Fiber <1 g; Sod 395 mg

ASIAN-STYLE MARINADE

From Lahey Clinic Executive Chef John R. Di Sessa, C.E.C.

■

INGREDIENTS

3/4　cup hoisin sauce

3/4　cup sherry

1/4　cup rice wine vinegar

1/4　cup soy sauce

4　garlic cloves, minced

METHOD

■ Combine the hoisin sauce, sherry, wine vinegar, soy sauce and garlic in a bowl and mix well. Use as a marinade for meat or fish. Be sure to marinate in the refrigerator.

Yield: 4 (1/2-cup) servings

Approx Per Serving: Cal 158; Prot 3 g; Carbo 24 g; T Fat 2 g; 10% Calories from Fat; Chol 1 mg; Fiber 1 g; Sod 2095 mg

BARBECUE MARINADE

From Lahey Clinic Executive Chef John R. Di Sessa, C.E.C.

■

INGREDIENTS

1　cup plus 2 tablespoons canola oil or olive oil

1/2　cup plus 2 tablespoons cider vinegar

2　tablespoons Worcestershire sauce

1　tablespoon brown sugar

2　teaspoons dry mustard

1　teaspoon Tabasco sauce

1　teaspoon garlic powder

1　teaspoon onion powder

2　garlic cloves, minced

METHOD

■ Combine the canola oil, vinegar, Worcestershire sauce, brown sugar, dry mustard, Tabasco sauce, garlic powder, onion powder and garlic in a bowl and mix well. Use as a marinade for meat or fish. Be sure to marinate in the refrigerator.

Yield: 4 (1/2-cup) servings

Approx Per Serving: Cal 576; Prot 1 g; Carbo 8 g; T Fat 62 g; 94% Calories from Fat; Chol 0 mg; Fiber <1 g; Sod 93 mg

African Vegetable Stew over Couscous

INGREDIENTS

2	medium onions, chopped	1/2	teaspoon (or less) salt
1	tablespoon vegetable oil	1/2	teaspoon pepper
1	pound boneless skinless chicken breasts, cubed	1/2	teaspoon ginger
		1/2	teaspoon turmeric
1	pound yellow squash or zucchini, sliced	1/2	teaspoon cumin
1	(16-ounce) can no-salt-added tomatoes, drained	1	(16-ounce) can no-salt-added garbanzos, drained, rinsed
2	carrots, coarsely chopped	2	cups medium grain couscous
1	green bell pepper, chopped	1	cup boiling water

METHOD

■ Sauté the onions in the oil in a stockpot. Add the chicken, squash, tomatoes, carrots, green pepper, salt, pepper, ginger, turmeric and cumin. Add just enough water to cover and mix well.

■ Cook, covered, until the chicken is cooked through and the vegetables are of the desired degree of crispness, stirring occasionally. Stir in the beans. Cook just until heated through, stirring occasionally.

■ Combine the couscous, boiling water and 1 cup of the broth from the chicken vegetable stew in a bowl and mix well. Let stand, covered, for 5 minutes. Fluff with a fork. Spoon into a serving bowl. Top with the chicken vegetable stew. You may substitute turnips or sweet potatoes for the squash.

Yield: 5 servings

Approx Per Serving: Cal 531; Prot 35 g; Carbo 82 g; T Fat 7 g; 12% Calories from Fat; Chol 50 mg; Fiber 11 g; Sod 307 mg

Apricot Citrus Chicken

■

INGREDIENTS

2	medium oranges
1/2	cup all-fruit apricot spread
1/4	cup unsweetened orange juice
2	teaspoons Dijon mustard
2	teaspoons cornstarch
1	tablespoon finely chopped gingerroot
2	garlic cloves, finely chopped
1 1/2	pounds boneless skinless chicken breasts, cut into 1/4-inch strips
3	cups hot cooked rice

METHOD

■ Peel the oranges. Separate each orange into sections, discarding the white pithy membrane. Whisk the apricot spread, orange juice, Dijon mustard and cornstarch in a bowl.

■ Heat a large skillet sprayed with nonstick cooking spray over medium-high heat until hot. Add the gingerroot and garlic. Stir-fry for 30 seconds. Add the chicken.

■ Stir-fry for 4 minutes or until the chicken is cooked through. Transfer the chicken with a slotted spoon to a bowl, reserving the pan drippings. Cover the chicken to keep warm.

■ Stir the apricot spread mixture into the pan drippings. Bring to a boil, stirring constantly; reduce heat. Cook for 1 minute or until thickened, stirring constantly.

■ Add to the chicken and mix well. Stir in the orange sections. Spoon over the rice on a serving platter. Garnish with orange zest.

Yield: 6 servings

Approx Per Serving: Cal 313; Prot 26 g; Carbo 45 g; T Fat 3 g; 9% Calories from Fat; Chol 63 mg; Fiber 3 g; Sod 98 mg

---

■

When shopping, try to avoid foods made with coconut, palm, and hydrogenated oils because they are high in saturated fat. Buy tub margarine that lists liquid unsaturated oils as the first ingredient (i.e., liquid corn oil, liquid safflower oil, liquid sunflower oil, liquid cottonseed oil, liquid soy oil, olive oil, canola oil).[5]

Asian Chicken Pizza

■

INGREDIENTS

3/4 cup rice wine vinegar	8 ounces boneless skinless chicken
1/4 cup packed brown sugar	breasts, cut into bite-size pieces
1/4 cup reduced-sodium soy sauce	1/2 cup shredded reduced-sodium
2 tablespoons peanut butter	Swiss cheese
1 tablespoon minced gingerroot	1/4 cup shredded part-skim
1 tablespoon cornstarch	mozzarella cheese
1/2 teaspoon crushed red pepper	1 (12-inch) prepared pizza crust
3 garlic cloves, minced	

METHOD

■ Whisk the wine vinegar, brown sugar, soy sauce, peanut butter, gingerroot, cornstarch, red pepper and garlic in a bowl. Sauté the chicken in a nonstick skillet coated with nonstick cooking spray for 2 minutes. Remove the chicken to a platter.

■ Pour the vinegar mixture into the skillet. Bring to a boil over medium-high heat, stirring frequently. Cook for 6 minutes or until slightly thickened, stirring frequently. Return the chicken to the skillet. Cook for 1 minute or until the chicken is cooked through, stirring constantly.

■ Sprinkle the Swiss cheese and mozzarella cheese over the pizza crust. Top with the chicken mixture. Place the pizza on the bottom rack of the oven. Bake at 500 degrees for 12 minutes or until brown and bubbly.

Yield: 6 servings

Approx Per Serving: Cal 308; Prot 18 g; Carbo 35 g; T Fat 9 g; 29% Calories from Fat; Chol 32 mg; Fiber <1 g; Sod 715 mg

BAKED CHICKEN WITH PEACHES IN ZINFANDEL SAUCE

From Lahey Clinic Executive Chef John R. Di Sessa, C.E.C.

■

INGREDIENTS

5   whole chicken breasts, split
1   cup apple cider
1½ tablespoons apple cider vinegar
1   tablespoon minced shallots
1   teaspoon minced garlic
9   ounces fresh peaches, peeled, sliced
2   cups fond de veau lié (reduced veal stock)
3½ tablespoons red zinfandel

METHOD

■ Arrange the chicken in a single layer in a shallow dish. Combine the apple cider, vinegar, shallots and garlic in a bowl and mix well. Pour over the chicken, turning to coat. Marinate in the refrigerator for 30 minutes, turning occasionally.

■ Drain the chicken, discarding the marinade. Arrange the chicken in a single layer in a baking pan. Bake at 350 degrees for 30 minutes or until the juices run clear and a meat thermometer registers 180 degrees. Let rest for several minutes.

■ Combine the peaches, fond de veau lié and wine in a saucepan. Bring to a simmer over low heat, stirring occasionally. Remove from heat. Cover to keep warm.

■ Remove the breast meat from the bones, discarding the skin and bones. Arrange on a serving platter. Serve with the warm wine sauce.

Yield: 10 servings

Approx Per Serving: Cal 171; Prot 28 g; Carbo 6 g; T Fat 3 g; 16% Calories from Fat; Chol 73 mg; Fiber <1 g; Sod 226 mg Nutritional information includes the entire amount of marinade.

■

To reduce the fat in your diet, use cooking methods that add little or no fats to foods. Cook meats on racks that drain away fats, and drain fat from the pan before making gravy. Season vegetables with herbs, spices, and lemon juice rather than fats and salt.[6]

CHICKEN BREASTS WITH SHERRY MUSHROOM SAUCE

■

INGREDIENTS

1	(10-ounce) can reduced-sodium chicken broth	1/8	teaspoon salt
4	(4-ounce) boneless skinless chicken breasts	2	cups sliced fresh mushrooms
2	tablespoons flour	2	tablespoons minced shallots
1/4	teaspoon pepper	1	tablespoon margarine
		1/4	cup dry sherry
		2	tablespoons chopped fresh parsley

METHOD

■ Bring the broth to a boil in a saucepan over high heat. Boil for 5 minutes or until reduced to 1 cup.

■ Heat a skillet coated with nonstick cooking spray over medium-high heat until hot. Coat the chicken with a mixture of the flour, pepper and salt. Add the chicken to the skillet. Cook for 5 minutes per side or until brown. Remove the chicken to a platter. Wipe the skillet with a paper towel.

■ Sauté the mushrooms and shallots in the margarine in the skillet over medium-high heat until the mushrooms are light brown. Stir in the sherry. Bring to a boil. Add the broth and mix well.

■ Cook for 7 minutes or until the sauce is reduced to 1 1/4 cups, stirring frequently. Return the chicken to the skillet; reduce heat. Simmer, covered, for 10 minutes or until the chicken is cooked through, stirring occasionally. Remove the chicken with a slotted spoon to a platter. Cover to keep warm.

■ Cook the mushroom sauce over high heat for 5 minutes or until reduced to 1 cup, stirring frequently. Stir in the parsley. Spoon 1/4 cup of the sauce over each chicken breast.

Yield: 4 servings

Approx Per Serving: Cal 196; Prot 25 g; Carbo 6 g; T Fat 6 g; 29% Calories from Fat; Chol 64 mg; Fiber 1 g; Sod 205 mg

CHICKEN WITH CASHEWS

INGREDIENTS

1	egg white
1	teaspoon cornstarch
1	teaspoon soy sauce
1/8	teaspoon white pepper
4	(6-ounce) boneless skinless chicken breasts, cut into 1/4-inch pieces
2	tablespoons olive oil or peanut oil
1	medium onion, cut into 8 wedges
1	teaspoon finely chopped gingerroot
1	(8-ounce) can bamboo shoots, drained, cut into 1/2-inch pieces

2	tablespoons olive oil or peanut oil
1	large green bell pepper, cut into 3/4-inch pieces
1	tablespoon hoisin sauce
2	teaspoons chili paste
1/4	cup chicken broth
1	tablespoon cornstarch
1	tablespoon cold water
1	tablespoon soy sauce
1/2	cup dry-roasted cashews
2	tablespoons chopped green onions and tops

METHOD

- Whisk the egg white, 1 teaspoon cornstarch, 1 teaspoon soy sauce and white pepper in a glass bowl. Add the chicken and toss to coat. Marinate, covered, in the refrigerator for 20 minutes.
- Heat a wok over medium-high heat until hot. Add 2 tablespoons olive oil, rotating the wok to coat the side. Add the chicken. Stir-fry until the chicken turns white. Remove the chicken to a platter. Add the onion and gingerroot. Stir-fry until the gingerroot is light brown. Stir in the bamboo shoots. Add 2 tablespoons olive oil, rotating the wok to coat the side.
- Return the chicken to the wok. Add the green pepper, hoisin sauce and chili paste and mix well. Stir-fry for 1 minute. Stir in the broth. Bring to a boil. Stir in a mixture of 1 tablespoon cornstarch, cold water and 1 tablespoon soy sauce. Cook for 20 to 30 seconds or until thickened, stirring constantly. Stir in the cashews and green onions.

Yield: 6 servings

Approx Per Serving: Cal 309; Prot 27 g; Carbo 12 g; T Fat 17 g; 50% Calories from Fat; Chol 63 mg; Fiber 2 g; Sod 452 mg

CHICKEN PICCATA

INGREDIENTS

4   (4-ounce) boneless skinless chicken breasts
3   tablespoons flour
1   teaspoon paprika
1   tablespoon margarine
2   tablespoons dry white wine
2   tablespoons lemon juice
1/4 teaspoon chicken bouillon granules
▪   Lemon wedges

METHOD

▪ Pound the chicken 1/4 inch thick between sheets of waxed paper with a meat mallet. Coat the chicken with a mixture of the flour and paprika.

▪ Spray a nonaluminum skillet with nonstick cooking spray. Add the margarine. Heat over medium-high heat until melted. Add the chicken. Cook for 6 to 8 minutes or until the chicken is brown and cooked through. Remove the chicken with a slotted spoon to a platter, reserving the pan drippings. Cover the chicken to keep warm.

▪ Stir the white wine, lemon juice and bouillon granules into the pan drippings. Cook for 30 seconds, stirring constantly. Drizzle over the chicken. Top with lemon wedges.

Yield: 4 servings

Approx Per Serving: Cal 176; Prot 24 g; Carbo 5 g; T Fat 6 g; 29% Calories from Fat; Chol 63 mg; Fiber <1 g; Sod 160 mg

CHEDDAR-STUFFED CHICKEN

INGREDIENTS

4	(4-ounce) boneless skinless chicken breasts	1	cup reduced-sodium chicken broth
3	ounces Cheddar cheese, cut into bite-size pieces	1	garlic clove, minced
		2	medium Granny Smith apples, peeled, cut into wedges
2	tablespoons flour	1	tablespoon honey
2	teaspoons vegetable oil	■	Sprigs of fresh rosemary
1	cup apple cider		

METHOD

■ Cut a horizontal slit through the thickest portion of each chicken breast to form a pocket. Stuff each pocket with ¹/₄ of the cheese. Coat the chicken with the flour.

■ Cook the chicken in the oil in a nonstick skillet for 4 minutes per side or until cooked through. Remove the chicken with a slotted spoon to a serving platter, reserving the pan drippings. Cover the chicken to keep warm.

■ Stir the apple cider, broth and garlic into the pan drippings. Bring to a boil. Cook for 10 minutes or until thickened, stirring frequently. Add the apples and honey and mix well.

■ Cook for 5 minutes longer or until the apples are tender and coated with the sauce, stirring frequently. Spoon the apple sauce over the chicken. Top with the fresh rosemary.

Yield: 4 servings

Approx Per Serving: Cal 326; Prot 30 g; Carbo 24 g; T Fat 12 g; 34% Calories from Fat; Chol 86 mg; Fiber 2 g; Sod 216 mg

GRILLED CHICKEN BREASTS WITH SWEET POTATO CAKES

From Lahey Clinic Executive Chef John R. Di Sessa, C.E.C.

INGREDIENTS

1	cup apple cider
2	tablespoons apple cider vinegar
$^1/_2$	ounce shallots, minced
1	garlic clove, minced
5	to 6 cracked black peppercorns
10	(4-ounce) boneless skinless chicken breasts
1	recipe Sweet Potato Cakes (page 117)

METHOD

- Combine the apple cider, vinegar, shallots, garlic and peppercorns in a shallow dish and mix well. Add the chicken, turning to coat. Marinate, covered, in the refrigerator for 2 hours, turning occasionally.
- Drain the chicken, discarding the marinade. Grill over hot coals until the chicken is cooked through and a meat thermometer registers 180 degrees, turning once or twice. Serve with Sweet Potato Cakes.

Yield: 10 servings

Approx Per Serving: Cal 232; Prot 26 g; Carbo 23 g; T Fat 3 g; 13% Calories from Fat; Chol 63 mg; Fiber 1 g; Sod 199 mg Nutritional information includes the entire amount of marinade and the Sweet Potato Cakes.

Sweet Potato Cakes

∎

INGREDIENTS

12 ounces each Idaho potatoes and sweet potatoes, peeled, chopped, cooked

4 ounces bread crumbs

2 tablespoons nonfat mayonnaise

6 tablespoons skim milk

2 teaspoons capers, rinsed, chopped

1 1/2 teaspoons chopped fresh chives

1 1/2 teaspoons chopped fresh dillweed

3/4 teaspoon cracked black peppercorns

METHOD

∎ Press the hot Idaho potatoes and hot sweet potatoes through a ricer into a bowl. Let stand until cool. Stir in the remaining ingredients. Shape into 10 patties.

∎ Arrange patties on a baking sheet. Bake at 475 degrees until golden brown.

Yield: 10 servings

Approx Per Serving: Cal 97; Prot 3 g; Carbo 20 g; T Fat 1 g; 6% Calories from Fat; Chol <1 mg; Fiber 1 g; Sod 144 mg

Lime-Sauced Chicken

∎

INGREDIENTS

4 (4-ounce) boneless skinless chicken breasts

3/4 cup apple juice or apple cider

2 teaspoons cornstarch

1/2 teaspoon chicken bouillon granules

∎ Grated zest and juice of 1/2 lime

METHOD

∎ Brown the chicken in a skillet sprayed with nonstick cooking spray for 8 to 10 minutes or until cooked through. Remove the chicken to a cutting board. Cover to keep warm. Mix the remaining ingredients together and add to the skillet.

∎ Cook for 2 minutes or until thickened, stirring constantly. Cut the chicken diagonally into 1-inch slices. Arrange on a serving platter. Spoon the lime sauce over the chicken on a platter. Garnish with additional lime zest.

Yield: 4 servings

Approx Per Serving: Cal 151; Prot 23 g; Carbo 7 g; T Fat 3 g; 17% Calories from Fat; Chol 63 mg; Fiber <1 g; Sod 200 mg

MUSHROOM-STUFFED CHICKEN WITH MARSALA SAUCE

■

INGREDIENTS

4 (4-ounce) boneless skinless chicken breasts
1/2 teaspoon olive oil
2 cups chopped mushrooms
1 large garlic clove, minced
1/4 teaspoon freshly ground pepper
4 (1/2-ounce) slices smoked Cheddar cheese

1/2 teaspoon olive oil
3/4 cup reduced-sodium chicken broth
1/4 cup marsala
1 teaspoon cornstarch
1 teaspoon water
■ Sprigs of fresh thyme

METHOD

■ Cut a horizontal slit through the thickest portion of each chicken breast to form a pocket. Heat 1/2 teaspoon olive oil in a nonstick skillet over medium heat until hot. Add the mushrooms and garlic. Sauté for 3 minutes. Stir in the pepper. Stuff 1/4 of the mushroom mixture and 1 slice of cheese into each pocket.

■ Heat 1/2 teaspoon olive oil in the same skillet over medium-high heat. Add the chicken. Cook for 6 minutes per side or until the chicken is cooked through. Remove the chicken to a platter with a slotted spoon, reserving the pan drippings. Cover the chicken to keep warm.

■ Stir the broth and wine into the reserved pan drippings. Bring to a boil. Cook for 2 minutes or until reduced to 3/4 cup. Stir in a mixture of the cornstarch and water. Bring to a boil. Cook for 1 minute or until thickened, stirring constantly. Return the chicken to the skillet.

■ Simmer, covered, for 2 minutes or until heated through. Remove the chicken to a serving platter. Spoon the wine sauce over the chicken. Top with sprigs of fresh thyme.

Yield: 4 servings

Approx Per Serving: Cal 218; Prot 28 g; Carbo 5 g; T Fat 9 g; 35% Calories from Fat; Chol 71 mg; Fiber <1 g; Sod 183 mg

CHICKEN WITH PLUM SAUCE

∎

INGREDIENTS

6	boneless skinless chicken breasts
1/4	teaspoon pepper
1/3	cup plum preserves
1/4	cup finely chopped onion
2	tablespoons frozen orange juice concentrate
1	tablespoon soy sauce
1	teaspoon prepared mustard
1/2	teaspoon ginger
1/4	cup dry white wine
1	tablespoon cornstarch
1	tablespoon cold water
1/2	teaspoon chicken bouillon granules

METHOD

∎ Sprinkle the chicken with the pepper. Mix the preserves, onion, orange juice concentrate, soy sauce, prepared mustard and ginger in a nonstick skillet.

∎ Simmer for 10 minutes, stirring occasionally. Stir in the white wine. Add the chicken, turning to coat. Simmer for 10 to 15 minutes or until the chicken is cooked through, spooning the plum sauce over the chicken occasionally. Transfer the chicken with a slotted spoon to a serving platter, reserving the sauce.

∎ Skim the excess fat from the sauce. Discard all but 1 cup of the sauce. Return the 1 cup sauce to the skillet. Stir in a mixture of the cornstarch, cold water and bouillon granules.

∎ Cook until thickened, stirring constantly. Remove the chicken with a slotted spoon to a serving platter. Drizzle with some of the plum sauce. Serve the remaining sauce with the chicken.

Yield: 6 servings

Approx Per Serving: Cal 363; Prot 54 g; Carbo 16 g; T Fat 6 g; 16% Calories from Fat; Chol 146 mg; Fiber <1 g; Sod 455 mg Nutritional information includes the entire amount of plum sauce.

∎

Proteins help regulate body processes. For example, as enzymes and hormones, they make various chemical reactions happen. As antibodies, they protect you from disease-carrying bacteria and viruses. When you consume more protein than you need, it's broken down and stored as body fat, not as a reserve supply of protein.[4]

Chicken Cheese Chiles Rellenos

Ingredients

3 (4-ounce) cans whole green chiles, drained

1 (4-ounce) can chopped green chiles, drained

2 large tomatoes, seeded, chopped

2 tablespoons minced onion

1 tablespoon chopped fresh cilantro

1 tablespoon white wine vinegar

1/2 cup chopped onion

2 garlic cloves, finely chopped

1 1/2 cups chopped cooked boneless skinless chicken breasts

1/2 cup shredded reduced-fat Monterey Jack cheese

1/4 teaspoon salt

1/4 teaspoon pepper

2 tablespoons reduced-fat mayonnaise

1 teaspoon water

1 1/2 cups dry bread crumbs

Method

■ Make a horizontal slit in each of 8 whole chiles to form a pocket. Discard the seeds. Chop the remaining whole chiles.

■ Combine the chopped whole chiles, canned chopped chiles, tomatoes, 2 tablespoons onion, cilantro and wine vinegar in a bowl and mix well. Chill, covered, in the refrigerator.

■ Sauté 1/2 cup onion and garlic in a nonstick skillet coated with nonstick cooking spray until the onion is tender. Stir in the chicken, cheese, salt and pepper. Spoon 1/4 cup of the chicken mixture into each whole chile.

■ Combine the mayonnaise and water in a bowl and mix well. Dip the stuffed chiles in the mayonnaise mixture. Coat with the bread crumbs.

■ Arrange the breaded chiles in a single layer on a baking sheet sprayed with nonstick cooking spray. Bake at 450 degrees for 10 to 12 minutes or until golden brown. Serve with the chilled tomato mixture.

Yield: 8 servings

Approx Per Serving: Cal 185; Prot 14 g; Carbo 22 g; T Fat 5 g; 23% Calories from Fat; Chol 27 mg; Fiber 2 g; Sod 1007 mg

Much Quicker Lasagna

■

INGREDIENTS

4	ounces ground turkey
4	cups prepared marinara sauce
3/4	cup water
8	ounces no-cook lasagna noodles
1	cup reduced-fat cottage cheese
3	ounces part-skim mozzarella cheese, sliced
1/4	cup freshly grated Parmesan cheese

METHOD

■ Brown the ground turkey in a nonstick skillet, stirring until crumbly; drain. Stir in the marinara sauce and water. Bring to a boil, stirring frequently. Remove from heat.

■ Spread 1/3 of the ground turkey mixture in a 9×13-inch baking dish. Layer 1/2 of the noodles, 1/2 of the cottage cheese and 1/2 of the mozzarella cheese over the prepared layer. Top with 1/2 of the remaining ground turkey mixture, remaining noodles, remaining cottage cheese and remaining mozzarella cheese. Spread with the remaining ground turkey mixture. Sprinkle with the Parmesan cheese.

■ Bake, covered, at 375 degrees for 1 hour. Let stand for 5 to 10 minutes before serving.

Yield: 6 servings

Approx Per Serving: Cal 370; Prot 22 g; Carbo 46 g; T Fat 12 g; 28% Calories from Fat; Chol 29 mg; Fiber 1 g; Sod 1360 mg

---

■

Polyunsaturated fatty acids are fatty acids missing two or more hydrogen pairs on their chemical chains. Foods high in polyunsaturated fatty acids are liquid or soft at room temperature. Corn, safflower, soybean, and sunflower oils are high in polyunsaturated fatty acids. Fat in seafood is mainly polyunsaturated.[4]

CHICKEN STOCK

INGREDIENTS

1	(3-pound) chicken	1	bay leaf
1	large onion	4	sprigs of parsley, or 1 tablespoon parsley flakes
2	ribs celery with leaves, cut crosswise into halves	1	teaspoon tarragon
2	carrots, coarsely chopped	1/2	teaspoon dillweed
4	cloves	1/2	teaspoon thyme
1	large garlic clove	12	black peppercorns

METHOD

■ Combine the chicken, onion, celery, carrots, cloves, garlic, bay leaf, parsley, tarragon, dillweed, thyme and peppercorns in a stockpot with enough cold water to cover. Bring to a boil; reduce heat.

■ Simmer, partially covered, for 1 hour. Remove the chicken to a platter. Cool slightly. Remove the chicken from the bones, reserving the meat for another purpose. Return the bones to the stockpot. Simmer for 1 hour longer.

■ Pour the stock through a strainer, sieve or cheesecloth into a bowl, discarding the solids. Chill and spoon off the hardened fat.

Yield: 8 (1-cup) servings

Approx Per Serving: Cal 35; Prot 8 g; Carbo 0 g; T Fat 0 g; 0% Calories from Fat; Chol 0 mg; Fiber 0 g; Sod 75 mg

FISH PIE

From the recipe files of Dr. Sara M. Jordan. Modified by
Lahey Clinic Executive Chef John R. Di Sessa, C.E.C.

■

INGREDIENTS

4   mushrooms, chopped
1/4 cup minced onion
1   teaspoon minced celery
1   tablespoon olive oil
1 1/2 cups 1% milk, scalded
1   tablespoon water
2   teaspoons cornstarch
■   Salt and white pepper to taste
1 3/4 cups coarsely chopped steamed cod
3   medium potatoes, peeled, steamed, cut into quarters
1/4 cup seasoned bread crumbs
1   teaspoon minced fresh parsley

METHOD

■ Sauté the mushrooms, onion and celery in the olive oil in a
saucepan for 5 minutes or until the onion is tender. Stir in
the 1% milk. Bring to a boil, stirring occasionally. Add a
mixture of the water and cornstarch and mix well.

■ Cook until thickened, stirring constantly. Season with salt
and white pepper. Fold in the cod and potatoes. Cook for
5 minutes, stirring frequently. Spoon into a baking dish.
Sprinkle with the bread crumbs.

■ Bake at 400 degrees until golden brown and a meat
thermometer registers 165 degrees. Sprinkle with the
parsley and garnish with lemon and lime twists.

Yield: 4 servings

*Approx Per Serving: Cal 249; Prot 20 g; Carbo 31 g; T Fat 5 g;
19% Calories from Fat; Chol 35 mg; Fiber 2 g; Sod 287 mg*

■

*While food choices don't
cause diabetes, diet is part
of the strategy for
managing diabetes, along
with physical activity and
perhaps medication. To
control blood sugar levels,
people with diabetes
manage the overall
carbohydrate, protein, and
fat in their diets. In the
past, people with diabetes
were warned to avoid or
strictly limit sugar in their
food choices. Today, experts
recognize that sugars and
starches have similar effects
on blood sugar levels.[4]*

BAKED HADDOCK NEW ENGLAND-STYLE

From the recipe files of Dr. Sara M. Jordan.
Modified by Lahey Clinic Executive Chef John R. Di Sessa, C.E.C.

■

INGREDIENTS

1	teaspoon margarine	1/4	cup sliced green onions
1	(3 1/2-pound) haddock, cleaned (head and tail removed)	2	tablespoons chopped fresh parsley
■	Pepper to taste	1/8	teaspoon pepper
1	tablespoon lemon juice	1/4	cup (1/2 stick) margarine, melted
1/2	cup salted cracker crumbs	2	tablespoons lemon juice
1/2	cup chopped fresh mushrooms	■	Sprigs of fresh parsley
		■	Lemon wedges

METHOD

■ Line a 9×13-inch baking sheet with foil. Coat the foil with 1 teaspoon margarine. Remove the bones from the fish with a sharp knife, keeping the fish joined down the back, or have your local butcher bone the fish.

■ Sprinkle the inside of the fish with pepper to taste. Drizzle with 1 tablespoon lemon juice. Arrange the fish on the prepared baking sheet.

■ Combine the cracker crumbs, mushrooms, green onions, chopped parsley and 1/8 teaspoon pepper in a bowl and mix well. Add 1/4 cup margarine and 2 tablespoons lemon juice and toss to mix. Spoon over the fish in a 3-inch-wide layer.

■ Bake at 400 degrees for 30 to 35 minutes or until the fish flakes easily, basting every 10 minutes with the pan juices. Remove the fish carefully to a heated serving platter. Top with sprigs of parsley and lemon wedges.

Yield: 6 servings

Approx Per Serving: Cal 362; Prot 56 g; Carbo 6 g; T Fat 11 g; 29% Calories from Fat; Chol 166 mg; Fiber <1 g; Sod 367 mg

Herb-Crusted Haddock

■

INGREDIENTS

1/4	cup flour
■	Salt and pepper to taste
1	cup bread crumbs
1	tablespoon chopped fresh parsley
1	tablespoon chopped fresh thyme, or 1/2 teaspoon dried thyme
1	cup 1% milk
1	egg
2	pounds haddock fillets
1 1/2	tablespoons margarine or butter
1/2	cup white grape juice
■	Lemon wedges

METHOD

■ Mix the flour, salt and pepper on a sheet of waxed paper. Mix the bread crumbs, parsley and thyme on another sheet of waxed paper. Whisk the 1% milk and egg in a shallow dish.

■ Coat the fillets with the flour mixture. Dip in the egg mixture and coat with the bread crumb mixture. Arrange the fillets in a dish. Chill, covered, for 30 to 40 minutes.

■ Heat the margarine in a large nonstick skillet over medium heat until melted. Add the fillets. Sauté until brown on both sides. Transfer to a greased baking dish. Pour the grape juice over the fillets. Bake at 375 degrees for 15 minutes or until the fish flakes easily. Top with lemon wedges.

Yield: 5 servings

Approx Per Serving: Cal 349; Prot 41 g; Carbo 27 g; T Fat 7 g; 20% Calories from Fat; Chol 149 mg; Fiber 1 g; Sod 389 mg

■

Seafood has less total fat and less saturated fat than meat and poultry. So eating fish regularly may help lower blood cholesterol levels. Seafood also provides several vitamins and minerals.[4]

Sauteed Halibut with White Beans, Orzo and Porcini

From Lahey Clinic Executive Chef John R. Di Sessa, C.E.C.

■

Ingredients

1	cup dried small white beans	■	Salt and pepper to taste
1/2	cup orzo	2	tablespoons olive oil
2	ounces dried porcini mushrooms	4	(6-ounce) fillets halibut or firm white fish
4	large tomatoes		
8	large unpeeled garlic cloves	2	teaspoons olive oil
3	tablespoons olive oil	1	teaspoon sherry wine vinegar
1	tablespoon sherry wine vinegar	2	tablespoons chopped fresh herbs of choice
1/2	cup chopped fresh herbs of choice		

Method

■ Sort and rinse the beans. Combine the beans with enough water to cover by 3 inches in a saucepan. Let stand for 8 to 10 hours; drain. Add enough water to generously cover the beans. Bring to a boil; reduce heat. Cook for 45 minutes or until almost tender, stirring occasionally. Stir in the orzo. Cook for 10 minutes longer or until the beans and orzo are tender; drain. Transfer to a bowl.

■ Combine the mushrooms with enough boiling water to cover in a heatproof bowl. Let stand for 30 minutes or until softened. Drain and chop the mushrooms.

■ Arrange the tomatoes and garlic in a baking pan. Bake the garlic at 400 degrees for 15 minutes or until roasted. Bake the tomatoes for 30 minutes or until the skins are blistered. Cool slightly. Peel and coarsely chop the tomatoes and place in a bowl. Squeeze the garlic into a bowl and mash. Stir the garlic into the tomatoes.

■ Stir the mushrooms and tomato mixture into the bean mixture. Whisk 3 tablespoons olive oil and 1 tablespoon wine vinegar in a small bowl until blended. Pour over the hot bean mixture. Stir in 1/2 cup herbs, salt and pepper. Let stand until room temperature. Heat 2 tablespoons olive oil in a heavy skillet over medium-high heat until hot. Season the fillets with salt and pepper. Sauté in the hot olive oil for 3 minutes per side or just until the fish flakes easily.

■ Divide the bean mixture equally among 4 dinner plates. Arrange the fish on top of the bean mixture using a slotted spoon. Drizzle with 2 teaspoons olive oil and 1 teaspoon wine vinegar. Sprinkle with 2 tablespoons herbs. Serve immediately.

Yield: 4 servings

Approx Per Serving: Cal 810; Prot 42 g; Carbo 66 g; T Fat 43 g; 47% Calories from Fat; Chol 71 mg; Fiber 18 g; Sod 151 mg

BAKED ORANGE ROUGHY

■

INGREDIENTS

2   pounds orange roughy fillets
1/3 cup plain nonfat yogurt
1   tablespoon lemon juice
2   teaspoons minced lemon zest
1   garlic clove, finely chopped
4   slices oat bran bread, crumbled
2   tablespoons grated Parmesan cheese
2   teaspoons olive oil

METHOD

■ Arrange the fillets in a single layer in a dish. Combine the yogurt, lemon juice, lemon zest and garlic in a bowl and mix well. Pour over the fillets, turning to coat.

■ Marinate, covered, in the refrigerator for 1 to 3 hours, turning occasionally.

■ Combine the bread crumbs, cheese and olive oil in a shallow dish. Coat the fillets with the crumb mixture. Arrange the fillets on a lightly greased broiler rack in a broiler pan.

■ Bake at 400 degrees for 10 minutes. Broil 4 to 5 inches from the heat source for 2 to 3 minutes; turn. Broil for 1 minute longer or until the fish flakes easily.

Yield: 6 servings

Approx Per Serving: Cal 178; Prot 25 g; Carbo 10 g; T Fat 4 g; 21% Calories from Fat; Chol 31 mg; Fiber 1 g; Sod 220 mg Nutritional information includes the entire amount of marinade.

■

Substitute nonfat or reduced-fat sour cream, plain nonfat yogurt, or Mock Sour Cream (page 67) for sour cream. Substitute Mock Cream Cheese (page 21) or Yogurt Cheese (page 150) for cream cheese.[5]

GRILLED SALMON WITH PINEAPPLE MANGO SALSA

From Lahey Clinic Executive Chef John R. Di Sessa, C.E.C.

■

INGREDIENTS

2¹/₂ pounds salmon fillets
1 tablespoon lemon juice
1 teaspoon lime juice
2 teaspoons minced shallots

2 teaspoons minced garlic
¹/₂ teaspoon crushed black peppercorns
■ Pineapple Mango Salsa

METHOD

■ Cut the fillets into ten 3¹/₂-inch portions. Arrange the fillets in a single layer in a dish. Drizzle with the lemon juice and lime juice. Sprinkle with the shallots, garlic and peppercorns.

■ Marinate, covered, in the refrigerator. Grill the salmon over hot coals until the fish flakes easily. Serve immediately with the warm Pineapple Mango Salsa.

PINEAPPLE MANGO SALSA

■

INGREDIENTS

1 ounce shallots, chopped
2 teaspoons minced jalapeño chile
2 teaspoons minced gingerroot
3¹/₂ tablespoons margarine
1¹/₄ cups fresh orange juice

1¹/₄ pounds chopped fresh pineapple
1 mango, chopped
1 tablespoon chopped fresh mint
1 tablespoon chopped fresh basil
¹/₂ teaspoon curry powder

METHOD

■ Sauté the shallots, chile and gingerroot in the margarine in a saucepan just until the aroma is released. Stir in the orange juice.

■ Cook until slightly reduced, stirring frequently. Add the pineapple, mango, mint, basil and curry powder. Cook over low heat just until heated through, stirring frequently. Remove from heat; do not allow to simmer. Cover to keep warm.

Yield: 10 servings

Approx Per Serving: Cal 263; Prot 22 g; Carbo 15 g; T Fat 13 g; 44% Calories from Fat; Chol 68 mg; Fiber 1 g; Sod 100 mg

Grilled Salmon with Pineapple Mango Salsa

NEW ENGLAND CLAMBAKE

From Lahey Clinic Executive Chef John R. Di Sessa, C.E.C.

■

INGREDIENTS

2	dozen soft-shell clams	2	cups water
4	unshucked ears of sweet corn	4	small baking potatoes, sweet
2	(2¹/₂-pound) chickens, quartered		potatoes or yams
1	cup (2 sticks) margarine	4	small onions
2	(1¹/₄-pound) live lobsters (optional)	■	Lemon wedges

METHOD

■ Scrub the clams under cold water with a stiff brush to remove any grit. Trim the tops off the corn with scissors. Pull cornhusks back and remove the silk. Reposition the husks. Remove only the outer husks from the ears. Soak these husks in lightly salted water in a large bowl until needed.

■ Sauté the chicken in 2 tablespoons of the margarine in a skillet for 10 minutes or until golden brown on both sides, adding additional margarine as needed.

■ Lay the lobsters on a wooden board. Sever the spinal cord by inserting the point of a knife through the back of the shell where the body and tail come together; turn the lobster over. With a sharp knife, split the body of the lobster down the middle, cutting through the thin undershell just to the back shell and leaving the back shell intact. Discard the dark intestinal vein running down the center of the lobster, as well as the small sack below the head. Crack the large claws.

■ Place a wire rack or racks in the bottom of a 4-gallon or larger stockpot. Pour in the water. Arrange the potatoes and onions on the rack. Cover with some of the reserved cornhusks or rockweed. Layer with the lobster, clams, corn and more cornhusks. Top with the chicken and more cornhusks.

■ Steam, covered, over medium heat for 1¹/₄ hours or until the vegetables are tender. Remove the clams with a slotted spoon to a larger bowl. Remove the potatoes, onions, lobster and corn with a slotted spoon to a large platter. Pour the remaining broth from the stockpot into four 8-ounce bowls or cups and use as a dipping sauce. Heat the remaining margarine until melted. Serve along with the lemon wedges.

Yield: 4 servings

Approx Per Serving: Cal 1098; Prot 71 g; Carbo 50 g; T Fat 69 g; 56% Calories from Fat; Chol 174 mg; Fiber 6 g; Sod 735 mg
Nutritional information does not include salt for soaking cornhusks.

Shrimp with a Kick

■

INGREDIENTS

3	tablespoons ketchup
2	teaspoons reduced-sodium soy sauce
1	teaspoon vinegar
1	tablespoon cornstarch
1	teaspoon white wine
1/4	teaspoon baking soda
1	egg, lightly beaten
1	pound medium shrimp, peeled, deveined
2	tablespoons vegetable oil
1	cup finely chopped green onions
1	teaspoon minced gingerroot
1/2	teaspoon crushed red pepper
2	garlic cloves, minced
2	cups hot cooked brown rice

METHOD

■ Combine the ketchup, soy sauce and vinegar in a bowl and mix well. Combine the cornstarch, white wine, baking soda and egg in a shallow dish and mix well. Add the shrimp, tossing to coat. Chill, covered, for 25 minutes.

■ Heat a skillet over medium heat until hot. Add 1 tablespoon of the oil. Add the shrimp mixture. Stir-fry for 3 minutes. Remove to a platter. Add the remaining 1 tablespoon oil to the skillet. Stir in the green onions, gingerroot, red pepper and garlic.

■ Stir-fry for 1 minute. Add the ketchup mixture and mix well. Stir-fry until heated through. Stir in the shrimp mixture. Spoon over the brown rice on a serving platter. Serve immediately.

Yield: 4 servings

Approx Per Serving: Cal 289; Prot 19 g; Carbo 30 g; T Fat 10 g; 31% Calories from Fat; Chol 188 mg; Fiber 3 g; Sod 479 mg

■

To reduce fat in your diet, choose more often fresh fish and shellfish, plain frozen seafoods without sauce, and canned fish packed in water rather than canned fish packed in oil or fried seafoods. Choose more often dry peas and beans and less often nuts and seeds. As snacks, choose more often fresh or frozen fruits and vegetables and air-popped popcorn and less often pastries and deep-fried foods.[6]

SHRIMP FILLING FOR PASTA

From Lahey Clinic Executive Chef John R. Di Sessa, C.E.C.

■

INGREDIENTS

14	ounces deveined peeled shrimp
3	tablespoons part-skim ricotta cheese
1	tablespoon chopped fresh basil
1/4	teaspoon salt
1/8	teaspoon white pepper
1/2	teaspoon lemon or lime juice

METHOD

■ Process the shrimp in a food processor until of the consistency of a fine paste. Add the ricotta cheese. Pulse several times or just until blended.

■ Combine the shrimp mixture with the basil, salt and white pepper in a bowl. Stir in the lemon juice. The filling may be used as a stuffing for fresh ravioli, tortellini or any other filled pasta. Serve on a bed of red pepper coulis.

Yield: 4 (1/2-cup) servings

Approx Per Serving: Cal 88; Prot 16 g; Carbo 1 g; T Fat 2 g; 18% Calories from Fat; Chol 145 mg; Fiber <1 g; Sod 322 mg

Fettuccini with Seafood

■

Ingredients

4   medium plum tomatoes, seeded, chopped
1/3   cup clam juice
1/4   cup chopped flat-leaf parsley
1/4   cup olive oil
3   tablespoons lemon juice
1   teaspoon grated lemon zest
2   teaspoons chopped fresh dillweed
1/2   teaspoon salt
1/2   teaspoon pepper
2   quarts water
12   ounces medium shrimp, peeled, deveined
12   ounces sea scallops, cut into quarters
12   ounces fettuccini, cooked, drained

Method

■ Combine the tomatoes, clam juice, parsley, olive oil, lemon juice, zest, dillweed, salt, and pepper in a bowl and mix well.
■ Bring the water to a boil in a stockpot. Add the shrimp and scallops. Boil for 2 minutes or until the shrimp turn pink and the scallops are tender; drain. Stir the shrimp, scallops and pasta into the tomato mixture.

Yield: 6 servings

Approx Per Serving: Cal 334; Prot 21 g; Carbo 37 g; T Fat 12 g; 32% Calories from Fat; Chol 82 mg; Fiber 2 g; Sod 612 mg

Fish Marinade

■

3/4 cup olive oil
1/4 cup lemon juice
2 garlic cloves, minced
1 teaspoon salt
1 teaspoon pepper

■

Combine the olive oil, lemon juice, garlic, salt and pepper in a jar with a tight-fitting lid. Shake to mix. Pour over your favorite fish fillets. Marinate, covered, in the refrigerator until just before grilling or baking.

■

For variety, substitute dry white wine or white vermouth for the lemon juice and shallots for the garlic.

Yield: 1 cup

MEATLESS DISHES

Mean Green Calzones

INGREDIENTS

2	teaspoons dry yeast	8	ounces tofu, chopped
1	tablespoon sugar	8	ounces part-skim mozzarella cheese, shredded
1¼	cups lukewarm water		
2	cups whole wheat flour	½	cup reduced-fat cottage cheese
2	cups all-purpose flour	½	cup part-skim ricotta cheese
½	teaspoon salt	¼	cup grated Parmesan cheese
1	(10-ounce) package frozen chopped spinach, thawed	2	garlic cloves, crushed
½	cup minced scallions	■	Freshly ground pepper to taste

METHOD

■ Dissolve the yeast and sugar in the lukewarm water in a bowl. Stir in the whole wheat flour, all-purpose flour and salt. Knead on a lightly floured surface for 10 to 15 minutes. Let rise, covered, in a warm place for 1 hour or until doubled in bulk. Punch the dough down. Divide the dough into 8 equal portions. Roll each portion into a ¼-inch-thick circle on a lightly floured surface.

■ Steam the spinach and scallions just until the scallions are tender. Combine the spinach, scallions, tofu, mozzarella cheese, cottage cheese, ricotta cheese, Parmesan cheese, garlic and pepper in a bowl and mix well.

■ Spoon about ½ cup of the spinach filling onto half of each circle, leaving a ½-inch rim. Moisten the edges of the circles with water and fold over to enclose the filling. Crimp the edges with a fork.

■ Arrange the calzones on a baking sheet sprayed with nonstick cooking spray. Bake at 450 degrees for 15 to 20 minutes or until light brown.

Yield: 8 calzones

Approx Per Calzone: Cal 374; Prot 23 g; Carbo 52 g; T Fat 9 g; 21% Calories from Fat; Chol 25 mg; Fiber 6 g; Sod 444 mg

Mixed Vegetable Calzones

■

Ingredients

3	cups chopped peeled eggplant	1	tablespoon extra-virgin olive oil
1	cup chopped onion	1	cup crumbled feta cheese
8	ounces fresh mushrooms, chopped	1/2	cup chopped fresh basil
1 1/2	cups chopped zucchini	1	(16-ounce) loaf frozen white bread
1	cup chopped yellow bell pepper		dough, thawed
1/2	teaspoon pepper	1	egg white
1/4	teaspoon salt	1	tablespoon water

Method

■ Combine the eggplant, onion, mushrooms, zucchini, yellow pepper, pepper and salt in a bowl and mix well. Add the olive oil and toss to coat. Spread the vegetable mixture in a single layer on a baking sheet. Bake at 425 degrees for 45 minutes, stirring every 15 minutes. Transfer the vegetable mixture to a bowl. Add the feta cheese and basil and mix well.

■ Divide the bread dough into 8 equal portions. Cover with a tea towel to keep from drying out. Roll each portion into a 7-inch circle on a lightly floured surface, working with 1 portion at a time. Spoon about 1/2 cup of the vegetable mixture onto half of each circle. Moisten the edge of the dough with water and fold over to enclose the filling. Crimp the edge with a fork. Arrange on a baking sheet sprayed with nonstick cooking spray. Repeat the process with the remaining dough and vegetable mixture.

■ Whisk the egg white and water in a bowl until blended. Brush the calzones with the egg mixture. Bake at 375 degrees for 20 minutes or until golden brown. Remove to a wire rack. Serve warm or at room temperature.

Yield: 8 calzones

Approx Per Calzone: Cal 255; Prot 11 g; Carbo 37 g; T Fat 8 g; 28% Calories from Fat; Chol 17 mg; Fiber 4 g; Sod 607 mg

VEGETARIAN CHILI

■

INGREDIENTS

2	cups chopped onions
3/4	cup chopped red bell pepper
3/4	cup chopped green bell pepper
1	garlic clove, minced
1	tablespoon chili powder, or to taste
1	teaspoon Italian seasoning
1	teaspoon crushed red pepper, or to taste
1	teaspoon cayenne pepper, or to taste
1/2	teaspoon black pepper, or to taste
16	ounces silken tofu, drained, chopped
1	(16-ounce) can Great Northern beans, drained, rinsed
1	(15-ounce) can tomato sauce
1	(15-ounce) can kidney beans, drained, rinsed
1	(15-ounce) can black beans, drained, rinsed
1	(14-ounce) can no-salt-added diced tomatoes
5	teaspoons grated Parmesan cheese

METHOD

■ Spray a Dutch oven with nonstick cooking spray. Heat over medium-high heat until hot. Add the onions, red pepper and green pepper. Sauté for 10 minutes or until the vegetables are tender. Add the garlic.

■ Sauté for 30 seconds. Stir in the chili powder, Italian seasoning, crushed red pepper, cayenne pepper, black pepper, tofu, Great Northern beans, tomato sauce, kidney beans, black beans and undrained tomatoes. Bring to a boil; reduce heat.

■ Simmer, covered, for 10 minutes or until heated through, stirring occasionally. Ladle into chili bowls. Sprinkle with the cheese.

Yield: 5 servings

Approx Per Serving: Cal 417; Prot 28 g; Carbo 70 g; T Fat 5 g; 11% Calories from Fat; Chol 2 mg; Fiber 21 g; Sod 877 mg

HERBED VEGETABLE STEW

■

INGREDIENTS

1	onion, finely chopped	1/2	teaspoon basil
2	tablespoons margarine, melted	1/2	teaspoon oregano
1	(28-ounce) can diced tomatoes	■	Freshly ground pepper to taste
1	(16-ounce) can chick-peas	1	green bell pepper, finely chopped
1/2	butternut squash, peeled, coarsely chopped	1	(16-ounce) can white kidney beans
1	garlic clove, crushed	1/8	teaspoon sugar
1	bay leaf	1/2	cup finely chopped parsley

METHOD

■ Sauté the onion in the margarine in a saucepan until tender. Stir in the undrained tomatoes, undrained chick-peas, squash, garlic, bay leaf, basil, oregano and pepper. Bring to a boil; reduce heat to medium-low.

■ Cook, covered, for 10 minutes or until the squash is tender-crisp, stirring occasionally. Stir in the green pepper and undrained kidney beans. Cook, covered, for 5 minutes longer or until the green pepper is tender and the beans are heated through. Stir in the sugar. Discard the bay leaf. Sprinkle each serving with some of the parsley.

Yield: 6 servings

Approx Per Serving: Cal 229; Prot 8 g; Carbo 37 g; T Fat 6 g; 22% Calories from Fat; Chol 0 mg; Fiber 11 g; Sod 596 mg

EGGPLANT AND LENTIL BAKE

■

INGREDIENTS

1	cup dried lentils	2	cups chopped leeks
3	cups water	2	cups chopped carrots
1	tablespoon olive oil	2	cups no-salt-added tomato juice
1	tablespoon reduced-sodium soy sauce	1	tablespoon white wine vinegar
		1	tablespoon honey
1	tablespoon lemon juice	1/4	teaspoon salt
2	teaspoons paprika	1	(28-ounce) can no-salt-added whole tomatoes
1	teaspoon oregano		
2	garlic cloves, minced	1/2	cup dry bread crumbs
6	cups chopped eggplant	1/2	cup grated Parmesan cheese

METHOD

■ Sort and rinse the lentils. Combine with the water in a saucepan. Bring to a boil; reduce heat. Simmer for 45 minutes or until tender, stirring occasionally; drain.

■ Combine the olive oil, soy sauce, lemon juice, paprika, oregano and garlic in a bowl and mix well. Stir in the eggplant. Spread the eggplant mixture on a baking sheet sprayed with nonstick cooking spray. Bake at 375 degrees for 30 minutes.

■ Spray a nonstick skillet with nonstick cooking spray. Heat over medium-high heat until hot. Add the leeks and carrots. Sauté for 5 minutes or until light brown. Stir in the tomato juice, wine vinegar, honey and salt. Add the undrained tomatoes, breaking into small pieces with a fork. Bring to a boil. Stir in the lentils and eggplant mixture; reduce heat.

■ Simmer for 35 minutes or until thickened, stirring occasionally. Spoon the lentil mixture into 4 individual gratin dishes sprayed with nonstick cooking spray. Sprinkle with a mixture of the bread crumbs and cheese. Bake at 375 degrees for 10 minutes or until brown and bubbly.

Yield: 4 servings

Approx Per Serving: Cal 455; Prot 24 g; Carbo 75 g; T Fat 9 g; 17% Calories from Fat; Chol 10 mg; Fiber 19 g; Sod 691 mg

CHEESY BEAN ENCHILADAS

■

INGREDIENTS

1   tablespoon vegetable oil
1   tablespoon chili powder
1¹/₂ tablespoons flour
1¹/₂ cups water
1   teaspoon vinegar
¹/₂ teaspoon each garlic powder, onion powder and salt
¹/₄ teaspoon oregano
³/₄ cup canned refried beans
²/₃ cup shredded reduced-fat Cheddar cheese
1   medium onion, finely chopped
¹/₂ cup reduced-fat cottage cheese
8   corn tortillas, heated
¹/₃ cup shredded reduced-fat Cheddar cheese
¹/₄ cup nonfat sour cream
¹/₄ cup finely chopped green onions

METHOD

■ Mix the oil, chili powder and flour in a saucepan. Cook until of the consistency of a paste, stirring constantly. Add the water gradually, stirring until of the consistency of a smooth sauce. Stir in the vinegar, garlic powder, onion powder, salt and oregano. Bring to a boil; reduce heat. Simmer for 3 minutes, stirring occasionally.

■ Combine the refried beans, ²/₃ cup Cheddar cheese, onion and cottage cheese in a bowl and mix well. Spoon ¹/₄ cup of the bean mixture down the center of each tortilla. Roll to enclose the filling.

■ Arrange the filled tortillas seam side down in a baking dish. Drizzle with the sauce. Sprinkle with ¹/₃ cup Cheddar cheese. Bake at 350 degrees for 20 minutes or until heated through. Top with the sour cream and green onions.

Yield: 8 enchiladas

Approx Per Enchilada: Cal 171; Prot 10 g; Carbo 21 g; T Fat 6 g; 30% Calories from Fat; Chol 11 mg; Fiber 3 g; Sod 422 mg

■

Researchers tell us today that most cancers can be prevented. Cancer is a disease directly affected by lifestyle choices. Eating right, staying physically active, watching your weight, and not smoking could reduce your cancer risk by 60 to 70 percent.[3]

LENTIL LOAF

INGREDIENTS

2   cups drained cooked lentils
2   cups shredded reduced-fat Cheddar cheese
1   cup bread crumbs, toasted
1   small onion, finely chopped
1   tablespoon margarine, melted
$1/2$ teaspoon pepper
$1/2$ teaspoon thyme
1   egg, lightly beaten
1   tablespoon Dijon mustard
1   tablespoon honey

METHOD

■ Mash the lentils in a bowl. Stir in the cheese, bread crumbs, onion, margarine, pepper, thyme and egg. Shape into a loaf in a 5×9-inch loaf pan.

■ Bake at 350 degrees for 45 minutes. Drizzle with a mixture of the Dijon mustard and honey. Bake for 5 minutes longer.

Yield: 8 servings

Approx Per Serving: Cal 228; Prot 15 g; Carbo 23 g; T Fat 8 g; 32% Calories from Fat; Chol 42 mg; Fiber 4 g; Sod 372 mg

POLKA-DOT PASTA

INGREDIENTS

12 ounces vermicelli
2   red bell peppers, julienned
1   large onion, thinly sliced
3   cups sliced mushrooms
2   tablespoons olive oil
1   (16-ounce) can black beans, drained, rinsed
1   (16-ounce) can diced tomatoes

1   (15-ounce) can kidney beans
2   tablespoons capers, drained, rinsed
1/4 cup sliced black olives
1/2 teaspoon basil
1/4 teaspoon rosemary
1/4 teaspoon pepper
2   tablespoons grated nonfat Parmesan cheese

METHOD

- Cook the pasta using package directions, omitting the salt and fat; drain. Cover to keep warm.
- Sauté the red peppers, onion and mushrooms in the olive oil in a skillet until tender. Stir in the black beans, undrained tomatoes, undrained kidney beans, capers, black olives, basil, rosemary and pepper. Bring to a boil; reduce heat.
- Simmer for 30 minutes, stirring occasionally. Spoon over the pasta on a serving platter. Sprinkle with the cheese.

Yield: 6 servings

Approx Per Serving: Cal 429; Prot 18 g; Carbo 74 g; T Fat 7 g; 15% Calories from Fat; Chol 0 mg; Fiber 12 g; Sod 690 mg

Eggplant Fettuccini

Ingredients

8	ounces fettuccini
2	cups coarsely chopped peeled eggplant
2	cups sliced mushrooms
3/4	cup red burgundy
1/2	cup sun-dried tomato tidbits
1 1/2	teaspoons sugar
1	(28-ounce) jar reduced-sodium and reduced-fat tomato and herbs pasta sauce
1/4	cup chopped fresh parsley
1/4	cup freshly shredded Parmesan cheese

Method

- Cook the pasta using package directions, omitting the salt and fat; drain. Spray a nonstick skillet with nonstick cooking spray. Heat over medium-high heat until hot. Add the eggplant and mushrooms.
- Sauté for 3 minutes. Add the wine. Cook for 2 minutes, stirring frequently. Stir in the sun-dried tomato tidbits, sugar and pasta sauce.
- Simmer for 5 minutes, stirring frequently. Spoon over the pasta on a serving platter. Sprinkle with the parsley and cheese.

Yield: 4 servings

Approx Per Serving: Cal 331; Prot 13 g; Carbo 57 g; T Fat 4 g; 9% Calories from Fat; Chol 5 mg; Fiber 6 g; Sod 506 mg

Lasagna Roll-Ups

Ingredients

12	ounces lasagna noodles	2	teaspoons vegetable oil
1	(14-ounce) jar tomato basil pasta sauce	15	ounces part-skim ricotta cheese
1/2	cup water	1/4	cup grated Parmesan cheese
1	(10-ounce) package frozen chopped broccoli, thawed, drained	1/2	teaspoon salt
2	tablespoons minced onion	1	egg, beaten
		1	cup shredded reduced-fat mozzarella cheese

Method

- Cook the noodles using package directions, omitting the salt and fat; drain. Combine the pasta sauce and water in a bowl and mix well. Spread 3/4 of the mixture in a 7×11-inch baking dish.
- Press the broccoli to remove the excess moisture. Sauté the broccoli and onion in the oil in a saucepan for 5 minutes or until the onion is tender. Remove from heat. Stir in the ricotta cheese, Parmesan cheese, salt and egg.
- Spread some of the broccoli mixture on each noodle. Roll to enclose the filling. Arrange the rolls seam side down in the prepared baking dish. Drizzle with the remaining pasta sauce mixture. Sprinkle with the mozzarella cheese. Bake, loosely covered, at 375 degrees for 30 minutes or until bubbly.

Yield: 12 servings

Approx Per Serving: Cal 212; Prot 12 g; Carbo 26 g; T Fat 7 g; 28% Calories from Fat; Chol 36 mg; Fiber 2 g; Sod 281 mg

Vegetarian Lasagna

■

Ingredients

6	carrots, grated	3/4	cup grated Parmesan cheese
1	Vidalia onion, thinly sliced or chopped	2	eggs, lightly beaten
3	ribs celery, thinly sliced or grated	1	bunch fresh basil, thinly sliced, or 2 tablespoons pesto
2	or 3 garlic cloves, finely minced or crushed	1	(26-ounce) jar tomato basil pasta sauce
1	teaspoon olive oil	12	ounces no-cook lasagna noodles
1	or 2 eggplant, sliced	8	ounces reduced-fat mozzarella cheese, shredded
8	ounces fresh mushrooms, sliced	1	ounce Parmesan cheese, grated
1	teaspoon olive oil		
15	ounces part-skim ricotta cheese		
8	ounces reduced-fat mozzarella cheese, shredded		

Method

■ Sauté the carrots, onion, celery and garlic in 1 teaspoon olive oil in a nonstick skillet until tender. Remove to a bowl. Sauté the eggplant in a nonstick skillet sprayed with nonstick cooking spray until brown on both sides. Add to the carrot mixture and toss to mix. Sauté the mushrooms in 1 teaspoon olive oil in a nonstick skillet until all of the moisture has evaporated. Add to the carrot mixture and toss to mix.

■ Combine the ricotta cheese, 8 ounces mozzarella cheese, 3/4 cup Parmesan cheese, eggs and basil in a bowl and mix well.

■ Layer 1/2 of the pasta sauce, 1/2 of the noodles, ricotta cheese mixture, 8 ounces mozzarella cheese, remaining pasta, vegetable mixture and remaining pasta sauce in a 9×13-inch baking pan. Sprinkle with 1 ounce Parmesan cheese. Bake at 350 degrees for 45 minutes. Freeze for future use if desired. You may substitute bell peppers, broccoli, spinach and/or your favorite vegetables for the carrots, celery and onion.

Yield: 8 servings

Approx Per Serving: Cal 565; Prot 38 g; Carbo 59 g; T Fat 20 g; 32% Calories from Fat; Chol 112 mg; Fiber 8 g; Sod 751 mg

CREAMY FOUR-CHEESE MACARONI

■

INGREDIENTS

3   cups elbow macaroni
2²/3 cups 1% milk
¹/3 cup flour
³/4 cup shredded fontina cheese or Swiss cheese
¹/2 cup freshly grated Parmesan cheese
¹/2 cup shredded extra-sharp Cheddar cheese
3   ounces Velveeta cheese, shredded
¹/4 teaspoon salt
12 onion melba toast rounds, crushed
1   tablespoon reduced-fat margarine, softened

METHOD

■ Cook the macaroni using package directions, omitting the salt and fat. Whisk the 1% milk gradually into the flour in a saucepan until blended. Cook over medium heat for 8 minutes or until thickened, stirring constantly. Add the fontina cheese, Parmesan cheese, Cheddar cheese and Velveeta cheese.

■ Cook for 3 minutes or until blended, stirring frequently. Remove from heat. Stir in the macaroni and salt. Spoon into a 2-quart baking dish sprayed with nonstick cooking spray.

■ Combine the crushed toast rounds and margarine in a bowl and mix well. Sprinkle over the top. Bake at 375 degrees for 30 minutes or until brown and bubbly.

Yield: 8 (1-cup) servings

Approx Per Serving: Cal 371; Prot 18 g; Carbo 44 g; T Fat 13 g; 31% Calories from Fat; Chol 36 mg; Fiber 2 g; Sod 584 mg

■

Regular stick margarine and butter contain the same number of calories, about 36 calories per teaspoon.[4]

ORECCHIETTE WITH BROCCOLI RABE

From Lahey Clinic Executive Chef John R. Di Sessa, C.E.C.

INGREDIENTS

- 1/4 cup olive oil
- 4 garlic cloves, minced
- 12 ounces orecchiette or any shell pasta
- Salt to taste
- 1 pound broccoli rabe, trimmed, chopped
- 2/3 cup grated pecorino Romano cheese
- 1/3 cup grated Parmesan cheese
- Pepper to taste

METHOD

- Heat the olive oil in a small heavy saucepan over medium heat until hot. Add the garlic. Sauté for 1 minute or until the garlic begins to brown. Remove from heat.
- Cook the pasta in boiling salted water in a saucepan for 8 minutes or just until the pasta begins to soften, stirring occasionally. Add the broccoli rabe.
- Cook for 3 minutes longer or until the pasta is tender but firm, stirring occasionally; drain. Transfer the pasta mixture to a bowl. Drizzle with the undrained garlic mixture. Sprinkle with the Romano cheese and Parmesan cheese and toss to coat. Season with salt and pepper. Serve immediately.

Yield: 6 servings

Approx Per Serving: Cal 375; Prot 15 g; Carbo 46 g; T Fat 15 g; 35% Calories from Fat; Chol 16 mg; Fiber 1 g; Sod 254 mg

Pasta Primavera

INGREDIENTS

12 ounces spaghetti
1¹/₂ cups sliced fresh mushrooms
1 medium onion, cut into thin wedges
2 garlic cloves, finely chopped
1 tablespoon olive oil
2 cups broccoli florets
1¹/₂ cups sliced zucchini

¹/₂ cup green peas
1 cup julienned carrot
¹/₃ cup dry white wine
¹/₄ cup chopped fresh parsley
1 tablespoon chopped fresh basil
¹/₄ teaspoon salt
¹/₈ teaspoon pepper
¹/₂ cup grated Parmesan cheese

METHOD

■ Cook the spaghetti in boiling water in a saucepan for 10 to 12 minutes or until al dente; drain. Cover to keep warm.

■ Sauté the mushrooms, onion and garlic in the olive oil in a skillet over medium-high heat for 1 to 2 minutes. Add the broccoli, zucchini, peas and carrot and mix well. Sauté for 2 to 3 minutes longer.

■ Stir in the white wine, parsley, basil, salt and pepper. Simmer for 4 to 5 minutes or until the vegetables are tender-crisp, stirring frequently. Toss the vegetable mixture, spaghetti and cheese together in a bowl. Serve immediately.

Yield: 6 servings

Approx Per Serving: Cal 321; Prot 13 g; Carbo 52 g; T Fat 6 g; 17% Calories from Fat; Chol 7 mg; Fiber 4 g; Sod 275 mg

PASTA WITH RED PEPPER SAUCE

INGREDIENTS

16   ounces angel hair pasta
4   red bell peppers, chopped
2   carrots, finely chopped
1   tablespoon olive oil
2   cups canned tomatoes with purée
1/2 pear, peeled, chopped
1   tablespoon basil
     Salt and pepper to taste
     Minced garlic to taste
1/4 cup grated Parmesan cheese

METHOD

- Cook the pasta using package directions, omitting the salt and fat; drain. Cover to keep warm.
- Sauté the red peppers and carrots in the olive oil in a skillet for 4 to 5 minutes or until tender. Add the tomatoes, pear, basil, salt, pepper and garlic. Simmer for 45 minutes, stirring occasionally. Spoon over the pasta on a serving platter. Sprinkle with the cheese.

Yield: 8 servings

*Approx Per Serving: Cal 236; Prot 10 g; Carbo 42 g; T Fat 4 g;
14% Calories from Fat; Chol 2 mg; Fiber 4 g; Sod 463 mg*

PASTA WITH RICOTTA CHEESE AND FRESH HERBS

From Lahey Clinic Executive Chef John R. Di Sessa, C.E.C.

■

INGREDIENTS

15 ounces part-skim ricotta cheese
²/₃ cup skim milk
¹/₂ cup grated Parmesan cheese
1 cup chopped onion
2 teaspoons olive oil
2 garlic cloves, chopped

¹/₂ cup chopped fresh basil
¹/₄ cup chopped fresh chives or
   green onions
¹/₄ cup chopped fresh parsley
12 ounces fusilli, cooked, drained
■ Salt and pepper to taste

METHOD

■ Process the ricotta cheese, skim milk and Parmesan cheese in a food processor until smooth. Sauté the onion in the olive oil in a heavy skillet over medium heat for 5 minutes or just until the onion begins to brown. Add the garlic.

■ Sauté for 2 minutes. Stir in the ricotta cheese mixture, basil, chives and parsley. Cook for 5 minutes or just until heated through, stirring constantly. Add the pasta and mix well. Season with salt and pepper. Serve immediately.

Yield: 4 servings

Approx Per Serving: Cal 563; Prot 29 g; Carbo 76 g; T Fat 16 g; 26% Calories from Fat; Chol 43 mg; Fiber 3 g; Sod 390 mg

Butternut Squash-Stuffed Manicotti

■

Ingredients

12 manicotti shells, or 16 jumbo pasta shells
1 pound butternut squash, peeled, cubed
1/2 cup finely chopped onion
1 tablespoon minced garlic
1 tablespoon olive oil
8 ounces green cabbage, finely shredded

1 teaspoon light brown sugar
1/2 cup vegetable broth
1/4 cup part-skim ricotta cheese
1 tablespoon tamari
1 cup tomato sauce, heated
1/2 cup shredded part-skim mozzarella cheese

Method

■ Cook the pasta using package directions until al dente, omitting the salt and fat. Drain and rinse in cold water. Steam or boil the squash in a saucepan until tender; drain. Mash the squash in a bowl.

■ Sauté the onion and garlic in the olive oil in a skillet until the onion is tender. Add the cabbage and brown sugar and mix well. Cook until the cabbage is wilted, stirring constantly. Stir in the squash and broth.

■ Cook for 5 minutes, stirring frequently. Stir in the ricotta cheese and tamari. Remove from heat. Spoon the squash mixture into a pastry bag. Pipe into the manicotti, or fill using a spoon.

■ Pour the tomato sauce into a baking dish. Arrange the manicotti in a single layer in the prepared baking dish. Sprinkle with the mozzarella cheese. Bake at 325 degrees for 10 to 15 minutes or until the cheese melts and is light brown.

Yield: 4 servings

Approx Per Serving: Cal 366; Prot 16 g; Carbo 61 g; T Fat 9 g; 20% Calories from Fat; Chol 13 mg; Fiber 8 g; Sod 850 mg

Penne with Sun-Dried Tomatoes

INGREDIENTS

1	cup boiling water
1/2	cup sun-dried tomatoes
16	asparagus stalks, trimmed
1	(15-ounce) can vegetable broth
2	tablespoons cornstarch
1/2	teaspoon minced garlic
2	tablespoons olive oil
2	tablespoons chopped fresh basil
2	tablespoons chopped fresh parsley
1	tablespoon chopped fresh dillweed
1/2	teaspoon freshly ground pepper
12	ounces penne, cooked, drained
1/2	cup grated Parmesan cheese

METHOD

■ Pour the boiling water over the sun-dried tomatoes in a heatproof bowl. Let stand for 10 to 15 minutes. Drain and chop. Steam the asparagus just until tender-crisp; drain. Slice the asparagus into 1-inch pieces.

■ Combine 1/4 cup of the broth and cornstarch in a bowl and mix well. Bring the remaining broth to a boil in a saucepan. Stir in the cornstarch mixture. Cook until thickened, stirring constantly.

■ Sauté the garlic in the olive oil in a large nonstick skillet for 1 minute. Stir in the sun-dried tomatoes, basil, parsley, dillweed, pepper and asparagus. Sauté for 1 minute. Add the broth mixture and mix well.

■ Bring to a simmer, stirring constantly. Stir in the pasta. Cook just until heated through, stirring frequently. Spoon into a serving bowl. Sprinkle with the cheese.

Yield: 4 servings

Approx Per Serving: Cal 499; Prot 19 g; Carbo 77 g; T Fat 13 g; 23% Calories from Fat; Chol 10 mg; Fiber 4 g; Sod 695 mg

---

■

Phytochemicals are substances that plants naturally produce to protect themselves against viruses, bacteria, and fungi. They include hundreds of naturally occurring substances, including carotenoids, flavonoids, indoles, isoflavones, capsaicin, and protease inhibitors. Different plant foods supply different kinds and amounts of phytochemicals. Their exact role in promoting health is still uncertain. However, certain phytochemicals may help protect against some cancers, heart disease, and other chronic health conditions.[4]

GRILLED AND ROASTED VEGETABLE TERRINE

From Lahey Clinic Executive Chef John R. Di Sessa, C.E.C.

■

INGREDIENTS

4 large artichokes	2 large portobello mushrooms, stems removed
■ Juice of 1 lemon	
■ Coarse salt to taste	3 red bell peppers
10 (1/4-inch) lengthwise slices eggplant	3 yellow bell peppers
5 (1/4-inch) lengthwise slices zucchini	2 leeks
5 (1/4-inch) lengthwise slices yellow squash	1 recipe Herb Aspic (page 156)
	■ Salt and pepper to taste
1 recipe Balsamic Vinaigrette (page 156)	

METHOD

■ Trim and stem the artichokes, removing any blemished parts. Place the artichokes in a medium saucepan. Add enough cold water to cover. Stir in the lemon juice and coarse salt. Lay a heavy tea towel over the top of the saucepan and top with a heatproof plate to keep the artichokes submerged. Bring to a boil over high heat; reduce heat.

■ Simmer for 30 minutes or until tender; drain. Let stand until the artichokes can be easily handled. Trim off the leaves and scrape away the chokes with a teaspoon, leaving nicely shaped bottoms. Cover and reserve until needed.

■ Combine the eggplant, zucchini and yellow squash with 1/2 cup of the Balsamic Vinaigrette in a shallow dish and toss to coat. Marinate at room temperature for 1 hour. Combine the mushrooms with 1/2 cup of the Balsamic Vinaigrette in a shallow dish and toss to coat. Marinate at room temperature for 1 hour.

■ Grill the red and yellow peppers over hot coals or broil for 5 minutes or until blackened. Place in a sealable plastic bag and seal tightly. Let steam for 5 minutes or until the skins can be removed easily. Remove the skins. Split the bell peppers into halves, discarding the stems, seeds and membranes. Drain on paper towels. Chop the bell peppers coarsely, reserving each color separately.

■ Grill the eggplant, zucchini and yellow squash over hot coals until tender but not mushy, turning once. Place the eggplant, zucchini and yellow squash in 3 separate containers. Pour 1/4 cup of the Balsamic Vinaigrette over each vegetable and toss to coat. Arrange the mushrooms on a baking sheet. Roast at 350 degrees for 5 minutes.

Toss with ¼ cup of the Balsamic Vinaigrette in a bowl. Combine the artichoke bottoms with ¼ cup of the Balsamic Vinaigrette in a bowl and toss to coat.

- Trim the leeks of all green parts, root bases and any tough outer leaves. Rinse with cold water several times. Cut lengthwise to but not through the centers and open. Place the leeks in a steamer basket over boiling water in a saucepan. Steam, covered, for 10 to 12 minutes or until tender. Drain on paper towels.

- Spray a 4×4×12-inch terrine with nonstick cooking spray. Line with plastic wrap, allowing 2 to 3 inches of overhang. Pour ¼ cup of the Herb Aspic into the prepared terrine. Pour 1 cup of the Herb Aspic into a bowl to use for dipping the vegetables.

- Dip the eggplant slices 1 at a time into the aspic. Lay 2 slices over the bottom of the prepared terrine to cover. Lay 4 slices slightly overlapping on each long side, allowing them to cover the sides and to overhang the edges by about 2 inches. Pour in enough aspic to cover. Sprinkle with salt and pepper. Layer with the squash and zucchini, dipping each piece into the aspic as you layer. Follow with a layer of mushrooms. Push the vegetables down, followed by the addition of the aspic as needed. Top with ⅔ of the leeks, pushing down and adding aspic as needed. Sprinkle with salt and pepper.

- Dip the artichoke bottoms in the aspic. Press into the leek layer, seasoning with salt and pepper and adding aspic as needed to cover. Layer with the remaining leeks, pressing down the seasoning and adding additional aspic as needed. Layer the red peppers and yellow peppers ½ at a time over the prepared layers, dipping each piece in the aspic. Push the vegetables down, adding aspic as needed and sprinkling with salt and pepper.

- Push the vegetables down gently to force out any air pockets and to ensure that the aspic covers all the vegetables and fills in any holes. Fold the eggplant up and over the top, adding the remaining aspic to cover. Sprinkle with salt and pepper. Fold the plastic wrap over the top and seal tightly. Cut a small vent in the top and press to expel any air. Chill for 8 hours. Lift from the terrine by holding onto the plastic wrap. Cut crosswise into ½-inch slices using a serrated knife.

Yield: 6 servings

Approx Per Serving: Cal 687; Prot 12g; Carbo 44 g; T Fat 55 g; 69% Calories from Fat; Chol 0 mg; Fiber 14 g; Sod 318 mg

BALSAMIC VINAIGRETTE

■

INGREDIENTS

1¹/₂ cups olive oil
³/₄ cup balsamic vinegar

■ Coarse salt and pepper to taste

METHOD

■ Combine the olive oil, balsamic vinegar, coarse salt and pepper in a jar with a tight-fitting lid. Shake until mixed.

Yield: 9 (¹/₄-cup) servings

Approx Per Serving: Cal 346; Prot 0 g; Carbo 6 g; T Fat 36 g; 93% Calories from Fat; Chol 0 mg; Fiber 0 g; Sod 4 mg

HERB ASPIC

■

INGREDIENTS

4   cups vegetable stock
2¹/₂ tablespoons unflavored gelatin
■   Salt and pepper to taste
1   teaspoon minced fresh chervil

1   teaspoon minced fresh parsley
1   teaspoon minced fresh tarragon
1   teaspoon minced fresh thyme
1   teaspoon minced fresh chives

METHOD

■ Combine 1 cup of the stock with the gelatin in a saucepan and mix well. Let stand for 2 minutes or until softened. Cook over low heat for 1 minute or until the gelatin dissolves, stirring constantly.
■ Heat the remaining 3 cups stock in a saucepan just until warm. Whisk in the gelatin mixture until blended. Season with salt and pepper. Let stand until room temperature. Stir in the chervil, parsley, tarragon, thyme and chives.
■ Place 2 tablespoons of the aspic in a small bowl in an ice bath for several minutes. It should be melting soft but firm. Adjust seasonings as needed.

Yield: 4 (1-cup) servings

Approx Per Serving: Cal 28; Prot 4 g; Carbo 1 g; T Fat 1 g; 20% Calories from Fat; Chol 0 mg; Fiber <1 g; Sod 283 mg

Grilled and Roasted Vegetable Terrine

Vegetarian Whole Wheat Pizza

Ingredients

2 cups whole wheat flour	3/4 cup shredded reduced-fat Swiss cheese
1/4 cup wheat germ	1/3 cup grated Parmesan cheese
1 envelope dry yeast	1 recipe Homemade Tomato Sauce (page 159)
3/4 teaspoon salt (optional)	2 or 3 plum or small round tomatoes, thinly sliced lengthwise
1 cup water	
1 tablespoon vegetable oil	16 fresh basil leaves
1 tablespoon honey	1 small green bell pepper, julienned
1 pound fresh spinach, trimmed	1 small red bell pepper, julienned
1 garlic clove, finely minced	
1 tablespoon olive oil	
1 1/2 cups shredded part-skim mozzarella cheese	

Method

- Combine the whole wheat flour, wheat germ, yeast and salt in a bowl and mix well. Stir in the water, vegetable oil and honey.
- Rinse the spinach; do not drain. Cook, covered, in a saucepan for 3 minutes or until the spinach wilts. Place the spinach in a colander. Rinse with cold water; drain. Press the spinach to remove excess moisture; coarsely chop.
- Sauté the garlic in the olive oil in a skillet for 15 seconds; do not brown. Add the spinach and mix well. Cook for 1 minute, stirring constantly. Remove from heat.
- Spread the dough on a greased baking sheet. Toss the mozzarella cheese, Swiss cheese and Parmesan cheese in a bowl. Sprinkle 1 1/2 cups of the cheese mixture over the dough. Spread with the Homemade Tomato Sauce. Top with the spinach mixture. Arrange 3/4 of the tomato slices along the outer edge of the pizza, interspersing the slices with the fresh basil. Place the remaining tomato slices in a circle in the center of the pizza. Arrange the pepper strips in a similar fashion around the edge, alternating the red and green strips. Sprinkle with the remaining cheese mixture. Bake at 375 degrees for 20 to 25 minutes or until brown and bubbly. Let stand for 5 minutes before serving.

Yield: 8 servings

Approx Per Serving: Cal 310; Prot 17 g; Carbo 35 g; T Fat 13 g; 36% Calories from Fat; Chol 23 mg; Fiber 7 g; Sod 311 mg

HOMEMADE TOMATO SAUCE

■

INGREDIENTS

1	medium onion, sliced
1	garlic clove, finely minced
1	tablespoon olive oil
1	(16-ounce) can plum tomatoes
1/4	teaspoon sugar
1/8	teaspoon red pepper flakes
■	Freshly ground black pepper to taste

METHOD

■ Cook the onion and garlic in 1 tablespoon olive oil in a skillet over medium-low heat until tender but not brown, stirring constantly; reduce heat.

■ Add the undrained tomatoes to the garlic mixture, breaking the tomatoes into small pieces with a fork. Stir in the sugar, red pepper flakes and black pepper. Simmer for 30 minutes or until thickened, stirring occasionally.

Yield: 2 (1-cup) servings

Approx Per Serving: Cal 128; Prot 3 g; Carbo 16 g; T Fat 7 g; 46% Calories from Fat; Chol 0 mg; Fiber 3 g; Sod 338 mg

■

Healthy Substitutions: substitute 1 cup recommended margarine or 2/3 cup recommended oil, or a mixture of 1/3 cup oil and 2/3 cup fruit purée in baked goods for 1 cup butter or shortening. Low-fat or fat-free mayonnaise and Yogurt Cheese (page 150) may be used in place of mayonnaise.[5]

CREAMY SPINACH AND FETA TART

■

INGREDIENTS

1   (10-ounce) package frozen chopped
    spinach, thawed, drained
1   cup 1% cottage cheese
2/3 cup buttermilk
1/2 cup crumbled feta cheese
3   eggs
1/4 teaspoon pepper

1/3 cup chopped green onions
1   tablespoon chopped fresh oregano
1   large garlic clove, minced
6   sheets frozen phyllo pastry, thawed
2   tablespoons fine bread crumbs
1 1/2 cups 1/4-inch-thick slices
    plum tomatoes

METHOD

■ Press the spinach to remove the excess moisture. Process the cottage cheese,
  buttermilk, feta cheese, eggs and pepper in a blender until smooth. Add the
  spinach, green onions, oregano and garlic. Process until blended.

■ Unroll the phyllo and cover with waxed paper topped with a damp towel to
  prevent it from drying out. Working with 1 phyllo sheet at a time, lightly coat
  with nonstick cooking spray. Fold in half crosswise to form an 8 1/2×13-inch
  rectangle. Spray both sides lightly with nonstick cooking spray. Press the rectangle
  gently into a 9-inch pie plate sprayed with nonstick cooking spray, allowing the
  ends to extend over the edge of the pie plate. Repeat the procedure with the second
  sheet of phyllo, placing it across the first sheet in a crisscross pattern. Sprinkle
  1/2 tablespoon of the bread crumbs over the second sheet. Repeat the procedure
  with the remaining phyllo and remaining bread crumbs, continuing in a crisscross
  pattern and ending with the phyllo.

■ Fold the edges of the phyllo in to form a rim. Spoon the spinach mixture into the
  prepared pie plate. Arrange the tomato slices over the top. Bake at 350 degrees for
  55 minutes or until set and a knife inserted in the center comes out clean. Let
  stand for 10 minutes before serving.

Yield: 6 servings

*Approx Per Serving: Cal 198; Prot 14 g; Carbo 19 g; T Fat 7 g; 33% Calories from Fat;
Chol 120 mg; Fiber 2 g; Sod 504 mg*

VEGETARIAN TORTILLAS

■

INGREDIENTS

2	ripe avocados	2	cups thinly sliced zucchini
1	tablespoon fresh lemon juice	1	green bell pepper, finely chopped
1¹/₂	cups finely chopped onions	³/₄	teaspoon salt
5	garlic cloves, minced	¹/₂	teaspoon cumin
3	small dried jalapeño chiles, crumbled	¹/₄	teaspoon coriander
		12	(8-inch) whole wheat tortillas
2	teaspoons oregano	2	medium tomatoes, chopped
1	teaspoon basil	1¹/₂	cups shredded reduced-fat
2	tablespoons canola oil		Monterey Jack cheese

METHOD

■ Slice the avocados paper-thin into a bowl. Drizzle with the lemon juice. Sauté the onions, garlic, chiles, oregano and basil in the oil in a skillet over medium heat until the onions are tender. Stir in the zucchini, green pepper, salt, cumin and coriander.

■ Simmer until the vegetables are tender-crisp, stirring occasionally. Remove from heat. Spoon some of the vegetable mixture down the middle of each tortilla. Sprinkle with 1 tablespoon tomato and about 5 avocado slices. Sprinkle with the cheese. Roll to enclose the filling.

■ Arrange the filled tortillas seam side down in a greased baking pan. Bake, covered, at 375 degrees for 10 to 15 minutes or until heated through. Serve with nonfat sour cream and chunky salsa.

Yield: 12 tortillas

Approx Per Tortilla: Cal 208; Prot 9 g; Carbo 27 g; T Fat 11 g; 40% Calories from Fat; Chol 8 mg; Fiber 5 g; Sod 412 mg

DESSERTS

ORANGE CHIFFON CHEESECAKE

■

INGREDIENTS

2   cups graham cracker crumbs
¹⁄₄   cup (¹⁄₂ stick) reduced-fat
      margarine, melted
1   envelope unflavored gelatin
1   cup cold orange juice
12   ounces reduced-fat cream cheese,
      softened

1   cup part-skim ricotta cheese
12   envelopes artificial sweetener
2   cups reduced-fat whipped topping
2   medium oranges, seeded, chopped

METHOD

■ Combine the graham cracker crumbs and margarine in a bowl and mix well. Press
the crumb mixture over the bottom and halfway up the side of a 9-inch springform
pan sprayed with nonstick cooking spray. Bake at 350 degrees for 8 to 10 minutes
or until light brown.

■ Sprinkle the gelatin over the orange juice in a saucepan. Let stand for 1 minute.
Cook for 3 minutes over low heat or until the gelatin dissolves, stirring constantly.
Beat the cream cheese and ricotta cheese in a mixer bowl until blended. Stir in the
artificial sweetener and gelatin mixture until blended. Fold in the whipped topping.
Fold in the chopped oranges.

■ Spoon the cream cheese mixture into the prepared pan. Chill, covered, for 6 to
10 hours. Garnish with orange sections.

Yield: 16 servings

*Approx Per Serving: Cal 189; Prot 6 g; Carbo 21 g; T Fat 9 g; 44% Calories from Fat;
Chol 17 mg; Fiber 1 g; Sod 207 mg*

APPLE CRISP

■

INGREDIENTS

2   cups sliced peeled fresh apples
1   tablespoon lemon juice
1   teaspoon cinnamon
1/8 teaspoon nutmeg
1/2 cup rolled oats
1/4 cup packed brown sugar
2   tablespoons margarine, melted
2   cups frozen vanilla yogurt

METHOD

■ Combine the apples, lemon juice, cinnamon and nutmeg in a bowl and mix gently. Spoon into a baking dish sprayed with nonstick cooking spray.

■ Combine the oats, brown sugar and margarine in a bowl and mix well. Sprinkle the oat mixture over the prepared layer. Bake at 350 degrees for 30 to 35 minutes or until brown and bubbly. Top each serving with 1/2 cup vanilla yogurt.

Yield: 4 servings

Approx Per Serving: Cal 333; Prot 10 g; Carbo 55 g; T Fat 9 g; 24% Calories from Fat; Chol 45 mg; Fiber 2 g; Sod 127 mg

■

Increase your activity level by getting up thirty minutes earlier in the morning and taking a brisk walk to start your day. Park at the far end of the parking lot for a longer walk to your office. Or get off the bus one or two stops ahead of your destination. Then walk briskly to your office. What great ways to start off the day![4]

GRILLED BANANAS

From Lahey Clinic Executive Chef John R. Di Sessa, C.E.C.

■

INGREDIENTS

5	bananas, sliced diagonally	1¼ cups Caramel Sauce (page 167)	
3	tablespoons sugar	20 Almond Tiles (below)	
15	ounces vanilla ice cream		

METHOD

■ Toss the bananas with the sugar. Grill over hot coals until marked and heated through. Arrange the bananas on 10 dessert plates. Top with the ice cream. Drizzle each with 2 tablespoons of the Caramel Sauce. Serve each with 2 Almond Tiles.

Yield: 10 servings

Approx Per Serving: Cal 340; Prot 4 g; Carbo 55 g; T Fat 12 g; 32% Calories from Fat; Chol 35 mg; Fiber 2 g; Sod 53 mg

ALMOND TILES

■

INGREDIENTS

3	cups confectioners' sugar	¼	cup milk
2	cups almond paste	¾	cup egg whites, lightly beaten
1	cup bread flour		

METHOD

■ Process the confectioners' sugar, almond paste and bread flour in a food processor until of a fine granular consistency. Add the milk gradually, processing constantly. Add the egg whites gradually, processing constantly until smooth.

■ Transfer the dough to a bowl. Chill, covered, for 8 to 10 hours. Spread a thin layer of the dough over the surface of an inverted baking sheet. Bake at 375 degrees until the dough loses its gloss. Cut into desired shapes with a knife or pizza cutter.

Yield: 150 tiles

Approx Per Tile: Cal 27; Prot 1 g; Carbo 5 g; T Fat 1 g; 28% Calories from Fat; Chol <1 mg; Fiber <1 g; Sod 3 mg

CARAMEL SAUCE

■

INGREDIENTS

1 cup sugar
7 tablespoons water
6 tablespoons unsalted butter
1/2 cup evaporated skim milk
2 tablespoons rum
2 teaspoons arrowroot

METHOD

■ Combine the sugar, water and butter in a saucepan. Cook over medium heat until smooth and caramel in color, stirring constantly. Remove from heat.

■ Mix the evaporated skim milk, rum and arrowroot in a bowl. Add to the hot caramel mixture, stirring constantly until blended. Bring to a boil, stirring constantly. Remove from heat. Let stand until cool.

Yield: 12 (2-tablespoon) servings

Approx Per Serving: Cal 131; Prot 1 g; Carbo 18 g; T Fat 6 g; 39% Calories from Fat; Chol 16 mg; Fiber 0 g; Sod 13 mg

■

Healthy Substitutions: 1 egg white or 2 tablespoons egg substitute for 1 egg yolk, or 2 egg whites or 1/4 cup egg substitute for 1 whole egg.[5]

FRUITFUL FLAN

INGREDIENTS

1	cup sugar
2	(12-ounce) cans evaporated skim milk
3/4	cup egg substitute
1/3	cup sugar
3/4	teaspoon vanilla extract
1/4	cup sliced fresh strawberries
1/4	cup sliced kiwifruit
1/4	cup fresh blueberries
1/4	cup apple jelly, melted

METHOD

■ Heat 1 cup sugar in a heavy skillet over medium heat for 5 minutes or until the sugar melts; do not stir. Cook until golden brown, stirring constantly. Pour into a 9-inch flan pan, tilting the pan to coat the bottom.

■ Whisk the evaporated skim milk, egg substitute, 1/3 cup sugar and vanilla in a bowl until blended. Pour into the prepared pan. Place the flan pan in a larger baking pan. Add enough hot water to the larger pan to measure 1 inch.

■ Bake at 350 degrees for 1 hour or until a knife inserted near the center comes out clean. Remove the flan pan to a wire rack. Let stand for 1 hour. Chill, covered, for 4 hours. Run a sharp knife around the edge of the flan pan. Invert onto a serving platter, drizzling any remaining syrup from the pan over the flan. Arrange the strawberries, kiwifruit and blueberries in a decorative pattern over the top of the flan. Brush the fruit with the apple jelly.

■ To prepare as shown in the photograph, bake in individual flan molds. The baking time may be decreased; bake until the flan tests done.

Yield: 8 servings

Approx Per Serving: Cal 252; Prot 9 g; Carbo 52 g; T Fat 1 g; 4% Calories from Fat; Chol 3 mg; Fiber <1 g; Sod 145 mg

Fruitful Flan

169

Rum Flan

■

INGREDIENTS

1/4 cup sugar	1/3 cup sugar
2 1/4 cups skim milk	1/4 cup dark rum
1 (12-ounce) can evaporated milk	5 eggs
1 (5-inch) vanilla bean	

METHOD

■ Sprinkle 1/4 cup sugar in a heavy skillet. Cook over medium heat until the sugar melts and is of the consistency of a light brown syrup, stirring constantly. Pour into a flan pan, tilting the pan to cover the bottom.

■ Combine the skim milk, evaporated milk and vanilla bean in a saucepan. Cook over medium heat until bubbles form around the edge of the pan. Discard the vanilla bean. Whisk the sugar, rum and eggs in a bowl. Add the hot milk mixture to the egg mixture gradually, whisking constantly until blended. Pour into the prepared pan. Cover with foil.

■ Place the flan pan in a larger baking pan. Add enough hot water to the larger pan to measure 1 inch. Bake at 350 degrees for 1 1/2 hours or until a knife inserted near the center comes out clean.

■ Remove the flan to a wire rack; remove the foil and let cool. Chill, covered, for 8 hours. Run a knife around the edge of the pan. Invert onto a serving platter. Garnish with lemon zest or sprigs of fresh mint.

Yield: 8 servings

Approx Per Serving: Cal 200; Prot 9 g; Carbo 23 g; T Fat 6 g; 28% Calories from Fat; Chol 141 mg; Fiber 0 g; Sod 118 mg

Fruit Parfaits

■

INGREDIENTS

2   cups puréed watermelon
12 ounces peaches, peeled, sliced
8   ounces kiwifruit, coarsely chopped
3/4 cup fresh blueberries
20 red or green seedless grapes
2   tablespoons fresh lime juice
2   teaspoons finely grated gingerroot

METHOD

■ Combine the watermelon, peaches, kiwifruit, blueberries, grapes, lime juice and gingerroot in a bowl and mix gently. Chill, covered, for 30 minutes; stir.

■ Spoon the fruit mixture into 8 parfait glasses or goblets just before serving.

Yield: 8 servings

Approx Per Serving: Cal 73; Prot 1 g; Carbo 18 g; T Fat 1 g; 7% Calories from Fat; Chol 0 mg; Fiber 3 g; Sod 4 mg

■

Serve fruit for dessert. Slice a melon, mango, or papaya. Open a can of pineapple or tropical fruit salad. These sweet desserts will quickly take the top spot for after-meal choices.[2]

FRESH FRUIT TRIFLE

INGREDIENTS

1	(6-ounce) package vanilla instant pudding mix
1	(12-ounce) angel food cake
1/3	cup seedless raspberry jam
1	cup chopped fresh strawberries
1	cup chopped kiwifruit
1	cup chopped peeled peaches
1/2	cup fresh raspberries
1/2	cup fresh blueberries
1	tablespoon amaretto
1	cup nonfat vanilla yogurt
1	cup reduced-fat whipped topping

METHOD

- Prepare the pudding mix using package directions, substituting skim milk for the whole milk. Cut the angel food cake into 3/4-inch slices. Spread each slice with some of the jam. Toss the strawberries, kiwifruit, peaches, raspberries and blueberries gently in a bowl.
- Drizzle the amaretto around the inside of a 3-quart trifle bowl. Layer the cake, mixed fresh fruit and pudding 1/2 at a time in the trifle bowl. Fold the yogurt into the whipped topping in a bowl. Spread over the top. Chill, covered, for 2 hours or longer.

Yield: 12 servings

Approx Per Serving: Cal 240; Prot 6 g; Carbo 52 g; T Fat 1 g; 5% Calories from Fat; Chol 1 mg; Fiber 3 g; Sod 435 mg

SPICY GINGERBREAD WITH LEMON SAUCE

INGREDIENTS

1	teaspoon baking soda	¹/₂ teaspoon nutmeg
2	tablespoons hot water	¹/₂ teaspoon allspice
1	cup dark molasses	¹/₂ teaspoon cinnamon
¹/₂	cup packed brown sugar	1 cup boiling water
¹/₂	cup canola oil	2¹/₂ cups unbleached flour
1	teaspoon ginger	Lemon Sauce

METHOD

- Dissolve the baking soda in the hot water in a small bowl and mix well. Combine the molasses, brown sugar, canola oil, ginger, nutmeg, allspice and cinnamon in a bowl and mix well. Stir in the boiling water. Add the flour and mix well. Stir in the baking soda mixture.
- Spoon the batter into an 8×8-inch baking pan sprayed with nonstick cooking spray. Bake at 350 degrees for 30 minutes. Cool slightly. Cut into 12 squares. Drizzle each square with the warm Lemon Sauce.

LEMON SAUCE

INGREDIENTS

¹/₄ cup sugar	1¹/₂ teaspoons margarine
1¹/₂ teaspoons cornstarch	1¹/₂ teaspoons lemon juice
¹/₂ cup water	1¹/₂ teaspoons grated lemon zest

METHOD

- Combine the sugar and cornstarch in a saucepan and mix well. Add the water gradually, stirring constantly. Bring to a boil over medium heat, stirring constantly.
- Boil for 1 minute, stirring frequently. Stir in the margarine, lemon juice and zest. Serve warm.

Yield: 12 servings

Approx Per Serving: Cal 310; Prot 3 g; Carbo 53 g; T Fat 10 g; 28% Calories from Fat; Chol 0 mg; Fiber <1 g; Sod 124 mg

HOT FUDGE PUDDING DESSERT

■

INGREDIENTS

1	cup flour
3/4	cup sugar
3	tablespoons baking cocoa
2	teaspoons baking powder
1/4	teaspoon salt
1/2	cup skim milk
1/3	cup margarine, melted
1 1/2	teaspoons vanilla extract
1/2	cup sugar
1/2	cup packed brown sugar
1/4	cup baking cocoa
1 1/4	cups hot water

METHOD

■ Combine the flour, 3/4 cup sugar, 3 tablespoons baking cocoa, baking powder and salt in a bowl and mix well. Add the skim milk, margarine and vanilla, stirring until smooth. Spoon into a 9×9-inch baking pan.

■ Combine 1/2 cup sugar, brown sugar and 1/4 cup baking cocoa in a bowl and mix well. Sprinkle over the prepared layer. Pour the hot water over the top; do not stir.

■ Bake at 350 degrees for 40 minutes or until the center is almost set. Let stand for 15 minutes before serving. Spoon into dessert bowls.

Yield: 12 servings

Approx Per Serving: Cal 211; Prot 2 g; Carbo 40 g; T Fat 6 g; 23% Calories from Fat; Chol <1 mg; Fiber 1 g; Sod 198 mg

MERINGUE SHELLS WITH FRESH FRUIT

INGREDIENTS

6   egg whites
1   teaspoon vanilla extract
¹/₄ teaspoon cream of tartar
¹/₄ teaspoon salt
1   cup sugar
1   cup pineapple tidbits, chopped,
    chilled

1   cup chopped fresh strawberries,
    chilled
1   cup chopped kiwifruit, chilled
¹/₂ cup fresh raspberries, chilled
¹/₂ cup fresh blueberries, chilled

METHOD

- Line a baking sheet with nonrecycled brown paper. Draw ten 3-inch circles
  2 inches apart on the paper.
- Combine the egg whites, vanilla, cream of tartar and salt in a mixer bowl. Beat at
  medium speed until soft peaks form. Add the sugar gradually, beating constantly at
  high speed until stiff but not dry peaks form. Spoon into a pastry bag fitted with
  a star tip.
- Pipe the meringue into circles on the paper to form shells. Bake for 1 hour. Turn
  off the oven. Let the meringues stand in the oven for 1 hour.
- Toss the pineapple, strawberries, kiwifruit, raspberries and blueberries gently in a
  bowl. Place 1 meringue shell on each of 10 dessert plates. Spoon some of the fruit
  mixture into each shell.

Yield: 10 servings

*Approx Per Serving: Cal 145; Prot 3 g; Carbo 34 g; T Fat <1 g; 2% Calories from Fat;
Chol 0 mg; Fiber 3 g; Sod 94 mg*

BERRY MOUSSE

INGREDIENTS

2   cups thawed frozen unsweetened raspberries
1¹/₂ cups thawed frozen unsweetened strawberries
1   large package sugar-free raspberry gelatin
1   cup boiling water
¹/₂ cup reduced-fat sour cream
2   tablespoons lemon juice
1   pint frozen strawberry reduced-fat yogurt

METHOD

■ Process the undrained raspberries and undrained strawberries in a blender until puréed. Strain into a bowl, discarding the seeds.

■ Dissolve the gelatin in the boiling water in a heatproof bowl. Combine the gelatin, sour cream, lemon juice and yogurt in a blender container. Process until smooth. Add to the berry purée and mix gently.

■ Spoon into dessert bowls. Chill for 4 to 6 hours or until set. Garnish with nonfat whipped topping and chopped maraschino cherries.

Yield: 8 servings

Approx Per Serving: Cal 156; Prot 5 g; Carbo 29 g; T Fat 2 g; 12% Calories from Fat; Chol 8 mg; Fiber 3 g; Sod 99 mg

SWEET DREAM MOUSSE

■

INGREDIENTS

1	envelope unflavored gelatin	1	teaspoon vanilla extract
3/4	cup cold skim milk	1/2	cup thawed frozen strawberries
1	cup 1% cottage cheese	1/4	cup miniature semisweet
1	cup part-skim ricotta cheese		chocolate chips
1/2	cup sugar		

METHOD

■ Sprinkle the gelatin over 1/4 cup of the skim milk in a blender container. Let stand for 2 minutes. Bring the remaining 1/2 cup skim milk to a boil in a saucepan. Add to the blender container.

■ Process at low speed for 2 minutes or until the gelatin dissolves. Add the cottage cheese, ricotta cheese, sugar and vanilla. Process for 2 minutes longer or until blended. Pour equal amounts of the pudding into 2 bowls.

■ Process the undrained strawberries in a blender until puréed; strain. Stir into 1 bowl of the pudding. Chill both bowls, covered, for 3 hours or until set. Whisk each pudding separately until smooth. Stir the chocolate chips into the plain pudding. Spoon the pudding mixtures side-by-side into 6 stemmed dessert goblets.

Yield: 6 servings

Approx Per Serving: Cal 221; Prot 12 g; Carbo 29 g; T Fat 6 g; 26% Calories from Fat; Chol 15 mg; Fiber 1 g; Sod 223 mg

BAKED PEARS WITH GINGERSNAP CRUMBS

From Lahey Clinic Executive Chef John R. Di Sessa, C.E.C.

INGREDIENTS

4	pears, peeled, cut into halves
4	gingersnap cookies
1/4	cup honey
1/4	cup fresh lemon juice
1/2	teaspoon ginger

METHOD

■ Arrange the pears cut side up in a single layer in a shallow 1-quart baking dish. Crush the cookies between 2 sheets of plastic wrap with a rolling pin or heavy pan.

■ Combine the honey, lemon juice and ginger in a bowl and mix well. Drizzle over the pears. Sprinkle with the cookie crumbs.

■ Bake at 425 degrees for 10 minutes. Baste with the pan juices. Bake for 10 to 15 minutes longer or until the pears are tender when pressed with a skewer and the syrup has thickened. Serve warm or at room temperature, drizzling each pear half with some of the syrup.

Yield: 8 servings

Approx Per Serving: Cal 98; Prot 1 g; Carbo 25 g; T Fat 1 g; 6% Calories from Fat; Chol 0 mg; Fiber 2 g; Sod 23 mg

Poached Pear Fans with Raspberry Orange Sauce

From Lahey Clinic Executive Chef John R. Di Sessa, C.E.C.

■

INGREDIENTS

3	medium pears
2¼	cups water
1	cup orange juice

2	(4-inch) cinnamon sticks
■	Raspberry Orange Sauce
■	Sprigs of fresh mint

METHOD

■ Peel and core the pears, leaving the stems intact. Slice the pears lengthwise into halves, leaving the stem intact on 1 side.

■ Combine the water, orange juice and cinnamon sticks in a large saucepan and mix well. Bring to a boil; reduce heat. Add the pears. Simmer, covered, for 10 minutes or until the pears are tender. Remove from heat. Let stand in liquid until cool.

■ Transfer the pears with a slotted spoon to a cutting board. Arrange the pears cut side down. Cut lengthwise slits in the pears to within ½ inch of the stem end, forming a fan. Spoon ⅓ cup of the chilled Raspberry Orange Sauce onto each of 6 dessert plates. Arrange the pears over the sauce. Garnish with sprigs of mint.

Raspberry Orange Sauce

■

INGREDIENTS

2	(10-ounce) packages frozen raspberries in syrup, thawed
1	cup orange juice

1	tablespoon plus 1 teaspoon cornstarch
¼	teaspoon grated orange zest

METHOD

■ Process the undrained raspberries in a blender container until puréed. Strain into a bowl, discarding the seeds. Combine the orange juice, cornstarch and orange zest in a saucepan and mix well. Stir in the raspberry purée. Cook over medium heat until thickened, stirring constantly. Pour into a bowl. Chill, covered, until serving time.

Yield: 6 servings

Approx Per Serving: Cal 190; Prot 2 g; Carbo 48 g; T Fat 1 g; 3% Calories from Fat; Chol 0 mg; Fiber 6 g; Sod 2 mg

PEARS POACHED IN ZINFANDEL

From Lahey Clinic Executive Chef John R. Di Sessa, C.E.C.

■

INGREDIENTS

10	Bosc pears	$^1/_2$	ounce grated orange zest
$1^1/_4$ cups red zinfandel		1	cinnamon stick
4	ounces currant jelly	2	whole cloves
$^1/_4$	cup orange juice	$^1/_2$	teaspoon ginger

METHOD

■ Peel and core the pears, leaving the pears intact. Combine the pears, wine, jelly and orange juice in a saucepan. Combine the orange zest, cinnamon stick, cloves and ginger in a cheesecloth bag and tie securely. Add to the saucepan.

■ Bring to a simmer over medium heat. Simmer for 20 to 30 minutes or until the pears are tender. Taste the poaching liquid during the simmering process and discard the cheesecloth bag when the clove and cinnamon flavors are detected.

■ Remove the pears from the poaching liquid with a slotted spoon to a platter. Let stand until cool. Strain the poaching liquid into a shallow freezer dish. Freeze, stirring frequently during the freezing process to produce a slightly granular texture. Serve with the pears if desired.

■ You may substitute fresh peaches for the pears. Blanch the peaches in boiling water for 30 seconds to loosen the skins. Cut the peaches into halves and remove the pits. Poach for about 10 minutes.

Yield: 10 servings

Approx Per Serving: Cal 136; Prot 1g; Carbo 30 g; T Fat 1 g; 4% Calories from Fat; Chol 0 mg; Fiber 4 g; Sod 7 mg

One-Bowl Chocolate Mocha Cake

■

INGREDIENTS

1   tablespoon flour
3/4 cup plus 2 tablespoons flour
1/2 cup sugar
1/3 cup baking cocoa
1   teaspoon baking powder
1   teaspoon baking soda
1/2 teaspoon salt
1/2 cup packed light brown sugar
1/2 cup buttermilk
1   egg, lightly beaten
2   tablespoons vegetable oil
1   teaspoon vanilla extract
1/2 cup hot strong black coffee
1   tablespoon confectioners' sugar

METHOD

■ Spray a 9-inch round cake pan with nonstick cooking spray. Dust lightly with 1 tablespoon flour.

■ Combine 3/4 cup plus 2 tablespoons flour, sugar, baking cocoa, baking powder, baking soda and salt in a mixer bowl and mix well. Add the brown sugar, buttermilk, egg, oil and vanilla. Beat at medium speed for 2 minutes, scraping the bowl occasionally. Add the coffee. Beat until blended.

■ Spoon the batter into the prepared pan. Bake at 350 degrees for 30 to 35 minutes or until the edge pulls from the side of the pan. Cool in the pan on a wire rack for 10 minutes. Remove the cake to the wire rack. Let stand until cool. Sprinkle with the confectioners' sugar.

Yield: 12 servings

Approx Per Serving: Cal 142; Prot 2 g; Carbo 27 g; T Fat 3 g; 19% Calories from Fat; Chol 18 mg; Fiber 1 g; Sod 262 mg

■

Sugar adds more than sweetnes to cakes. Sugars contribute to the bulk, tenderness, smooth crumb texture, and lightly browned surface. In cakes that have air whipped in, such as angel food cakes and sponge cakes, sugars help hold the form.[4]

GUILTLESS CHOCOLATE CHIP COOKIES

INGREDIENTS

3   cups flour
1 1/2 teaspoons baking soda
1   teaspoon salt
1 1/4 cups packed dark brown sugar
1/2   cup sugar
1/2   cup (1 stick) margarine, softened
1   teaspoon vanilla extract
2   egg whites, or 1/4 cup egg substitute
1/3   cup water
2   cups semisweet chocolate chips
1/3   cup chopped walnuts (optional)
■   Grated orange zest (optional)

METHOD

■ Sift the flour, baking soda and salt together. Beat the brown sugar, sugar, margarine, vanilla and egg whites in a mixer bowl until creamy. Stir in the dry ingredients and water. Fold in the chocolate chips, walnuts and orange zest.

■ Drop the dough by spoonfuls 2 inches apart onto a cookie sheet sprayed with nonstick cooking spray. Bake at 350 degrees for 10 to 12 minutes or until light brown. Cool on the cookie sheet for 2 minutes. Remove to a wire rack to cool completely.

Yield: 5 dozen cookies

Approx Per Cookie: Cal 87; Prot 1 g; Carbo 14 g; T Fat 3 g; 32% Calories from Fat; Chol 0 mg; Fiber 1 g; Sod 92 mg

Oatmeal Raisin Chocolate Chip Cookies

■

Ingredients

3	cups rolled oats	1/2	teaspoon ground cloves
1/3	cup chopped pecans	1/4	teaspoon nutmeg
1	cup raisins	3/4	cup packed light brown sugar
1	cup water	3/4	cup sugar
2	cups flour	1/2	cup applesauce
1	teaspoon baking soda	2	eggs
1/2	teaspoon salt	1/4	cup canola oil
1/2	teaspoon baking powder	1	teaspoon vanilla extract
1/2	teaspoon cinnamon	1	cup semisweet chocolate chips

Method

■ Spread the oats and pecans on an ungreased baking sheet. Toast at 375 degrees for 5 to 7 minutes or until light brown, stirring occasionally. Combine the raisins and water in a saucepan. Bring to a simmer over low heat. Simmer for 10 minutes or until the raisins are plumped; drain. Sift the flour, baking soda, salt, baking powder, cinnamon, cloves and nutmeg into a bowl and mix well.

■ Beat the brown sugar, sugar, applesauce, eggs, canola oil and vanilla in a mixer bowl for 5 minutes or until light and fluffy, scraping the bowl occasionally. Stir in the flour mixture. Stir in the oats, pecans, raisins and chocolate chips.

■ Drop the dough by rounded teaspoonfuls 2 inches apart onto a cookie sheet sprayed with nonstick cooking spray. Bake at 375 degrees for 8 to 10 minutes or until light brown. Cool on the cookie sheet for 2 minutes. Remove to a wire rack to cool completely.

Yield: 3 1/2 dozen cookies

Approx Per Cookie: Cal 125; Prot 2 g; Carbo 22 g; T Fat 4 g; 26% Calories from Fat; Chol 10 mg; Fiber 1 g; Sod 69 mg

OATMEAL FRUIT COOKIES

■

INGREDIENTS

1	cup water	1	egg, lightly beaten
3/4	cup raisins	1	teaspoon baking soda
3/4	cup chopped dates	1	teaspoon vanilla extract
1/2	cup (1 stick) margarine, melted	1/2	teaspoon cinnamon
1 1/3	cups flour	1/2	teaspoon nutmeg
2/3	cup rolled oats	1/8	teaspoon salt

METHOD

■ Combine the water, raisins and dates in a saucepan. Bring to a boil. Boil for 6 minutes, stirring occasionally. Stir in the margarine. Add the flour, oats, egg, baking soda, vanilla, cinnamon, nutmeg and salt and mix well.

■ Drop the dough by rounded teaspoonfuls 2 inches apart onto a nonstick cookie sheet. Bake at 325 degrees for 7 minutes. Cool on the cookie sheet for 2 minutes. Remove to a wire rack to cool completely.

Yield: 2 dozen cookies

Approx Per Cookie: Cal 100; Prot 2 g; Carbo 15 g; T Fat 4 g; 37% Calories from Fat; Chol 9 mg; Fiber 1 g; Sod 112 mg

BIBLIOGRAPHY

■

1. American Institute for Cancer Research. June 1998. *AICR Science News.* Washington, D.C.

2. American Institute for Cancer Research. 1998. *Moving Towards a Plant Based Diet.*

3. American Institute for Cancer Research (on line). From a notice for the AICR 9th Annual Research Conference, *Nutrition and Cancer Prevention: New Insights into the Role of Phytochemicals.* www.AICR.org.

4. Chronimed Publishing. 1996. *The American Dietetic Association's Complete Food and Nutrition Guide,* by Roberta Larson Duyff, MS, RD, CFCS.

5. Sodexho Marriott Services Publication #DS-8. *Guidelines for a Healthy Lifestyle.*

6. U.S. Department of Health and Human Services, Public Health Service National Institutes of Health (on line). *Diet, Nutrition and Cancer Prevention: The Good News.* www.hoptechno.com/book12.htm

Numbers preceding information sources correspond to the numbers at the end of sidebar text located throughout book.

■

A famous researcher once said that people could avoid many chronic diseases if they just had ten new recipes. These recipes would be healthy ones that taste great, are easy to make, and are packed with nutrients. They also would be low in animal and saturated fat, high in vitamins and minerals, high in fiber and phytochemicals—all the components of food that contribute to vitality. We have collected favorite recipes of people who are committed to eating foods that have all these attributes. We believe that if they like these recipes and find meals appetizing and satisfying, so will you!

We encourage you to try one new recipe each week, marking the ones you like in your cookbook, and refer back to them when you are wondering what to make for a meal or a snack. We hope that you will find at least ten new recipes in this collection that will improve your health!

NUTRITIONAL PROFILE GUIDELINES

■

The editors have attempted to present these recipes in a format that allows approximate nutritional values to be computed. Persons with dietary or health problems or whose diets require close monitoring should not rely solely on the nutritional information provided. They should consult their physician or a registered dietitian for specific information.

ABBREVIATIONS FOR NUTRITIONAL PROFILE

Cal — Calories
Prot — Protein
Carbo — Carbohydrates

T Fat — Total Fat
Chol — Cholesterol
Fiber — Dietary Fiber

Sod — Sodium
g — grams
mg — milligrams

Nutritional information for these recipes is computed from information derived from many sources, including materials supplied by the United States Department of Agriculture, computer databanks, and journals in which the information is assumed to be in the public domain. However, many specialty items, new products, and processed food may not be available from these sources or may vary from the average values used in these profiles. More information on new and/or specific products may be obtained by reading the nutrient labels. Unless otherwise specified, the nutritional profile of these recipes is based on all measurements being level.

■ Artificial sweeteners vary in use and strength so should be used "to taste," using the recipe ingredients as a guideline. Sweeteners using aspartame (NutraSweet and Equal) should not be used as a sweetener in recipes involving prolonged heating, which reduces the sweet taste. For further information on the use of these sweeteners, refer to the package.

■ Alcoholic ingredients have been analyzed for the basic information. Cooking causes the evaporation of alcohol, which decreases alcoholic and caloric content.

■ Buttermilk, sour cream, and yogurt are the types available commercially.

■ Cake mixes which are prepared using package directions include 3 eggs and ½ cup oil.

■ Chicken, cooked for boning and chopping, has been roasted, which yields the lowest caloric values.

■ Cottage cheese is cream-style with 4.2 percent creaming mixture. Dry curd cottage cheese has no creaming mixture.

■ Eggs are all large. To avoid raw eggs that may carry salmonella, as in eggnog or 6-week muffin batter, use an equivalent amount of commercial egg substitute.

■ Flour is unsifted all-purpose flour.

■ Garnishes, serving suggestions, and other optional information and variations are not included in the profile.

■ Margarine and butter are regular, not whipped or presoftened.

■ Milk is whole milk, 3.5 percent butterfat. Low-fat milk is 1 percent butterfat. Evaporated milk is whole milk with 60 percent of the water removed.

■ Oil is any type of vegetable cooking oil. Shortening is hydrogenated vegetable shortening.

■ Salt and other ingredients to taste as noted in the ingredients have not been included in the nutritional profile.

■ If a choice of ingredients has been given, the profile reflects the first option. If a choice of amounts has been given, the profile reflects the greater amount.

INDEX

TO YOUR HEALTH

Recipes for Healthy Living from Lahey Clinic

■

Lahey Clinic
Office of Philanthropy
41 Mall Road
Burlington, Massachusetts
01805-0105

Please send _____ copies of *To Your Health* @ $29.95 each $ _____

Postage and handling $5.00 each $ _____

TOTAL $ _____

Name
_____

Street Address
_____

City   State   Zip
_____

Telephone
_____

Method of Payment: [   ] VISA   [   ] MasterCard   [   ] American Express
                     [   ] Check payable to Lahey Clinic "To Your Health"

Account Number   Expiration Date
_____

Signature
_____

Photocopies will be accepted.

Lahey

CLINIC